The media's watching Vault!
Here's a sampling of our coverage.

"Unflinching, fly-on-the-wall reports... No one gets past company propaganda to the nitty-gritty inside dope better than these guys."
— *Knight-Ridder newspapers*

"Best way to scope out potential employers...Vault.com has sharp insight into corporate culture and hiring practices."
— *Yahoo! Internet Life*

"Vault.com has become a de facto Internet outsourcer of the corporate grapevine."
— *Fortune*

"For those hoping to climb the ladder of success, [Vault.com's] insights are priceless."
— *Money.com*

"Another killer app for the Internet."
— *New York Times*

"If only the company profiles on the top sites would list the 'real' information... Sites such as Vault.com do this, featuring insights and commentary from employees and industry analysts."
— *The Washington Post*

"A rich repository of information about the world of work."
— *Houston Chronicle*

VAULT
> the most trusted name in career information™

Does it matter who you are?

Or does it matter what you can do?

At Deloitte, our firm's success is measured by the quality of our team's insights and solutions. So, the more diverse our people's backgrounds and expertise, the better. With more than 120,000 professionals worldwide, sharing their unique perspectives across our functions, service lines and offices, we are uniquely positioned in the global marketplace to understand our clients' complex needs and exceed their expectations. Are you ready to be yourself and make a difference in everything you do?

Deloitte.

Audit . Tax . Consulting . Financial Advisory .

www.deloitte.com/us

VAULT CAREER GUIDE TO ACCOUNTING

VAULT CAREER GUIDE TO ACCOUNTING

**JASON ALBA, MANISHA BATHIJA,
MATTHEW THORNTON
AND THE STAFF OF VAULT**

© 2005 Vault Inc.

Library of Congress CIP Data is available.

ISBN 1-58131-328-4

Printed in the United States of America

ACKNOWLEDGMENTS

We are extremely grateful to Vault's entire staff for all their help in the editorial, production and marketing processes. Vault also would like to acknowledge the support of our investors, clients, employees, family, and friends. Thank you!

Jason and Manisha would like to thank their friends and family for their continued love and support, and to everyone who contributed in the writing of this guide.

Table of Contents

ON THE JOB   63

On the Job   65

Is There Life After Public Accounting?   83

ACCOUNTING EMPLOYERS   85

Visit the Vault Finance Career Channel at **www.vault.com/finance** — with
insider firm profiles, message boards, the Vault Finance Job Board and more.

VAULT CAREER LIBRARY   **xi**

RICE
MBA

IF IT WASN'T HARD, EVERYONE WOULD DO IT.
THE 'HARD' IS WHAT MAKES IT GREAT. *

" It was a challenge getting a degree from Columbia and playing ball. The Jones School is even more demanding than my engineering program at Columbia. You have to actually think and interpret using all your knowledge and experience—it requires a lot more in-depth thought. "

Parker Meeks, Rice MBA 2005, captain of his high school football team, was recruited by Columbia University to play football, which he did for four years. Parker came to Rice after graduating from Columbia in 2003 to pursue an MBA/ME, focusing in finance and nanotechnology.

"Rice is perfect for this combination due to its strong programs in both areas. I was intrigued by the nanotechnology program at Rice after reading about the work of Professor Richard Smalley that led to his winning the 1996 Nobel Prize in Chemistry. My immediate career goals are to get corporate finance experience in a large corporation, keep abreast of nanotechnology and, in 5 to 10 years, join or found a nanotechnology company as the head of business operations. My internship at ExxonMobil was a fantastic opportunity to develop the finance skills that I will need to accomplish these goals, and now I'm choosing among several very attractive offers in corporate finance."

The Rice MBA is second to none and more challenging than most. We're looking for a few outstanding seniors to join us directly after graduation. If you think you're up to the challenge of a truly rigorous business education, we'd like to learn more about you.

Visit us at jonesgsm.rice.edu or call 888.844.4773

APPENDIX   115

Visit the Vault Finance Career Channel at **www.vault.com/finance** — with
insider firm profiles, message boards, the Vault Finance Job Board and more.

VAULT CAREER LIBRARY   **xiii**

Audit Bureau of Circulations

The Audit Bureau of Circulations (ABC), the world's first and largest circulation auditing firm, has entry-level Field Auditor positions available throughout the US.

The Audit Bureau of Circulations was formed in 1914 when advertisers, advertising agencies and publishers wanted to establish ground rules for reporting circulation statistics. Enforcing those rules as well as providing standardized audited circulation information to buyers and sellers of print media advertising-for the sale of credibility-were ABC's goals.

Field auditors normally work at ABC publisher member's offices, conducting an on-site verification of their circulation claims. By applying standardized auditing procedures, field auditors are able to establish compliance with ABC's Bylaws & Rules, and render an opinion attesting to the fact.

Our ideal candidates will have:
•A strong desire to travel (100%) - No relocation necessary
•Strong analytical aptitude
•Spreadsheet proficiency
•A Bachelor's degree in a business related field
•Relevant business experience a plus
•Reliable transportation is required

Starting base salary is competitive plus overtime, and all travel expenses, including semimonthly flights home, are reimbursed. Other benefits-such as medical, dental, life and disability insurance, 401(k) savings plan, retirement plan, tuition reimbursement and comprehensive training programs demonstrates how much ABC cares for its people.

For immediate consideration, please send your resume and cover letter:
recruiting@accessabc.com

Equal Opportunity Employer.
Begin your future with the Audit Bureau of Circulations
Web Site: *www.accessabc.com*

INTRODUCTION

Overview of Accounting

Who would have thought that, of all the issues in the world, accounting would ever be foremost among hot-button discussion topics? Accounting? Boring accounting? A profession once derided in a famous "Monty Python" sketch as a "horrible debilitating disease" whose practitioners are "appallingly dull, unimaginative, timid, lacking initiative, spineless, easily dominated, no sense of humor and irrepressibly drab?" Interesting and intriguing? Never!

Yet in early 2002, accounting was pulled from the depths of business arcana, hotly deliberated by politicians and television pundits alike, and plastered on the front pages of the popular press. As a result of the Enron debacle, accounting has entered the public consciousness like never before.

Unfortunately, most of this exposure has cast a negative light on this noble profession. Awash with devastating revelations of shady partnerships, government cronyism, hidden debt, shredded documents and conflicts of interest, all under the oversight of Arthur Andersen, the Enron scandal has played out like a soap opera with accounting as a central storyline. Andersen's alleged role in the scandal has struck a blow to the profession's image that is sure to change public perception about accounting and its practitioners. (A recent Times Square billboard advertisement for whiskey mocked the profession with the caption, "Disappears faster than a Big Five accounting firm." Ouch!)

The Enron scandal has not only changed the perception of accountants in the eyes of the public, but will change the field of accounting as we know it. The government, the Securities and Exchange Commission (SEC) and other regulatory agencies are discussing how to make the accounting profession more reliable and to increase the respect of accounting professionals in the eyes of the public. Congressional committees are considering issues ranging from auditor conflict of interest to the regulation of the derivatives market. The SEC has pledged to reform accounting rules and get tough on fraud and audit oversight. The accounting world as we know it is changing.

Despite the historic implications of the Enron scandal, the accounting profession remains hale and hearty. The work of accountants will always be needed. External audits by public accountants will continue to be required for public companies, tax professionals will be there to interpret the complicated tax laws and companies will still need accountants to ensure the accuracy of their financial records. More importantly, the rising complexity of corporate activities, the growth of international business and the increased use of technology are combining to change the roles of accountants, creating new opportunities and spurring job growth for the profession.

If you're interested in this industry, it's important to understand what it's going to take to be successful if you choose to pursue a career as an accountant. There are ethical considerations (currently a hot topic with the media) as well as a vast job market with thousands of opportunities to be understood and dissected. This Vault guide will give you the inside scoop you need to evaluate the career opportunities in the field.

THE SCOOP

What is Accounting?

CHAPTER 1

What exactly is accounting, and why do we need it? Accounting is a system by which economic information is identified, recorded, summarized and reported for the use of decision makers.

So what does that mean?

Put simply, accounting is the language of business. An accounting system essentially tracks all of the activities of an organization, showing when and where money has been spent and commitments have been made. This aids decision making by allowing managers to evaluate organizational performance, by indicating the financial implications of choosing one strategy over another and by highlighting current weaknesses and opportunities. It allows managers to take a step back, look at the organization, and assess how it is doing and determine where it should be going.

Accounting, however, is not the exclusive domain of Big Business. In all likelihood, you have been managing your own personal accounting system for years – it's called your checking account. Every time you record an entry in your check ledger, you are acting like an accountant. Your check ledger is an accounting log of all of your deposit and withdrawal activities, helping you identify your cash inflows and outflows and letting you know how much money you have left in the bank. It lets you know where your money went and helps you make decisions on how to plan your future purchases and expenses. If this log is not regularly balanced for accuracy, you would have an inaccurate picture of your cash position and might spend more than you have (a common situation, given the popularity of overdraft protection features offered by banks).

You get the picture. Now, imagine these functions performed on more complicated items and on a much larger scale. While you might have 500 checkbook transactions in a year, many organizations might have that many transactions every minute. This is what an accountant does. And, just as you would eventually be lost without a relatively accurate checkbook, organizations would not be able to make useful decisions without an accurate accounting system. Anyone who has pulled out his or her hair trying to balance their checkbook should have an appreciation for both the importance and challenges of accounting.

Why Accounting?

So why would anyone choose a career in accounting as opposed to another business profession, like investment banking or management consulting? Isn't accounting boring and tedious?

As we discussed earlier, accounting has always had an image problem, stuck in the public consciousness as a profession populated by math geeks who love crunching numbers but little else. While this stereotype may have been accurate at one point in history, it no longer presents an accurate picture of what the career is like. While the basic mechanics of accounting can certainly become tedious, such functions are increasingly becoming automated, with accountants focusing more on analysis, interpretation and business strategy.

In fact, accounting has been rated one of the most desirable professions available. According to *The 2002 Jobs Rated Almanac*, "accountant" was the fifth best job in terms of low stress, high compensation, lots of autonomy and tremendous hiring demand. Furthermore, the *National Association of Colleges and Employers' Summer 2004 Salary Survey* ranked the accounting services industry first among the top ten employers with job offers for graduating college students.

Uppers and downers

Uppers

- **Collegial work environment.** Public accounting firms, particularly the Big Four firms (Deloitte Touche Tohmatsu, Ernst & Young, KPMG and PricewaterhouseCoopers; see sidebar on p. 10), tend to hire large classes of newly graduated accountants. Being surrounded by so many people with similar interests and concerns makes acclimation to the firm and the job much more agreeable. It also provides fertile ground for networking opportunities. According to one public accountant, "I started with a class of almost 100 other college graduates, and we bonded quickly through all of the training and client work. While most of these people have since left the firm, I still keep in touch with most of them, which is great since they've all fanned out to dozens of interesting companies. I've already turned some of them into clients and am working on many others. The networking opportunity is tremendous."

- **Applicability to many functions.** A strong knowledge of accounting is applicable across all management functions, including purchasing, manufacturing, wholesaling, retailing, marketing and finance. It provides a base from which to build broad knowledge about virtually all business functions and industries. As the collectors and interpreters of financial information, accountants develop comprehensive knowledge about what is occurring and close relationships with key decision makers, and are increasingly being called upon to offer strategic advice. Senior accountants or controllers are often selected as production or marketing executives because they have acquired in-depth general management skills.

- **Exposure to different companies.** Public accounting offers rapid exposure to a number of different clients and activities, accelerating the attainment of skills and experience. According to one Big Four audit senior who specializes in entertainment industry clients, "I've been with the firm for less than three years, but I've become intimately involved in work for large industry players like Sony, Viacom and Disney, as well as for a good number of smaller entertainment and media companies. Being able to learn about the business of entertainment from the industry's benchmark companies has really sped up my professional development. Few professions would have offered me such a great learning opportunity."

- **Better hours and less stress than investment banking and management consulting.** The hours and travel required by the accounting profession are much less stressful and more predictable than that found in investment banking and consulting. In public accounting, you generally know you'll be very busy for a few months out of the year and then settle in to a manageable 40- to 45-hour workweek, whereas I-bankers and consultants are notorious for regularly pulling 60-80 hour weeks (at least) and hopping on planes at a moment's notice. "As hard as I worked as an accountant, my life has truly been swallowed by my I-banking job," says one former auditor who, after attaining an MBA, is now an investment banker. "I pretty much work six days a week, with at least part of my Sunday spent on some work item or another. I actually had a life when I was an auditor – not anymore."

- **Great for women.** The profession has taken great strides to implement flexible work arrangements and other initiatives to provide lifestyle choices for women. According to the Bureau of Labor Statistics, women now account for approximately 60 percent of the accounting profession, with the outlook for women accountants looking bright. According to a CFO survey by Robert Half International, 58 percent of CFOs believe that the number of women accountants in management-level positions

Visit the Vault Finance Career Channel at **www.vault.com/finance** — with insider firm profiles, message boards, the Vault Finance Job Board and more.

VAULT CAREER LIBRARY

9

(such as vice president or chief financial officer) will increase in the next five years. According to one partner who has worked for several large firms, "At the risk of sounding politically incorrect, my 17 years of experience have shown me that women tend to make better accountants than men. In my observation, men often tend to be focused on the big picture, while women are more acutely aware of intricate detail. Well, accounting demands a detail-oriented approach more than any other skill, so you do the math."

The Big Four

When accountants speak of the Big Four, they're talking about the four largest accounting/professional services firms. The Big Four is comprised of Deloitte & Touche, Ernst & Young, KPMG and PricewaterhouseCoopers. All four are based in New York but have operations around the world. (The Big Four had been the Big Five prior to Arthur Andersen's conviction on federal obstruction of justice charges in June 2002. Andersen surrendered its license to audit public companies in the Unites States in August 2002 and has become a shell of its former self.) Here are the Big Four at a glance:

Deloitte Touche Tohmatsu
CEO: William G. Parrett
No. of Employees: 120,000
No. of Offices: 665

KPMG
CEO: Robert W. Alspaugh
No. of Employees: 98,000
No. of Offices: 715

Ernst & Young
CEO: James S. Turley
No. of Employees: 103,000
No. of Offices: 670

PricewaterhouseCoopers
CEO: Samuel A. DiPiazza, Jr.
No. of Employees: 120,000
No. of Offices: 768

Downers

- **Lower pay than investment banking and consulting.** The more manageable lifestyle has its tradeoff: lower pay. On average, starting base salaries in accounting are 15 to 20 percent lower than investment banking or consulting, not including the bonus incentives that can significantly increase a banker's or consultant's overall pay package. According to the same former auditor/current investment banker from above, "I do make a lot more money as an I-banker – I mean a LOT – which does make up somewhat for losing my personal life, but it doesn't feel that way all the time. Sometimes it seems that, if you divided my I-banking compensation by the number of hours I spend working, I would be making about minimum wage." Bonus incentives are much smaller in public accounting, if they exist at all. "You'll never become 'stinkin' rich' on an accountant's wage," adds one Big Four tax partner, "but I like to think that, since we are supposed to be conservative and intelligent in matters pertaining to money, we know best how to take care of our money and make it work for us. You will definitely lead a comfortable life."

• **Many bosses with different priorities.** Accountants, particularly public accountants, are usually assigned to multiple projects at any given time and must prioritize and, when needed, learn to say "no." This is particularly true in public accounting, where multiple, simultaneous projects for different clients are commonplace. According to one auditor, juggling projects "has honestly been the hardest part of my job. Forget the clients, they're relatively easy to deal with – it's the partners on those clients that get you. They all want you to focus on their projects first. On more than one occasion, a partner has screamed my head off, really got down and cursed, because of a perceived 'lack of focus' on my part. You just have to try to explain your situation, try to demonstrate that you have everything covered, and move on." However, this premium on time management is also present in investment banking and consulting.

• **Relatively conservative, conformist cultures.** Accountants are generally looking to see if reported numbers conform to one set of regulations or another (Generally Accepted Accounting Principles, the Internal Revenue Code, SEC regulations, etc.). This emphasis on regulations (in fact, one might say that the entire accounting industry exists *because of* regulations) translates into a generally risk-averse culture and ethos that emphasizes conformity

• **Pressure to stay "chargeable."** This is one of the subtler, yet highly sensitive parts of being an accountant. Like attorneys, public accountants generally work under billable hour arrangements (they are paid by clients for each hour billed). This means that they must account for every single hour they work and accurately allocate them to each project they work on, whether client-related or otherwise. Being "chargeable" means billing a high percentage of your hours to work performed for paying clients as opposed to non-billable projects. This tracking of billable hours, while often tedious, is absolutely crucial to the profession – it is the basis for how public accounting firms determine revenues, expenses, profitability, efficiency, performance and a host of other metrics. With such vital items at stake, timesheets and chargeability often are the subject of much stress and consternation.

Visit the Vault Finance Career Channel at **www.vault.com/finance** — with insider firm profiles, message boards, the Vault Finance Job Board and more.

VAULT CAREER LIBRARY   **1 1**

"Yeah, we can work 60 hours in a week," says one audit senior, "but not all of those hours are chargeable to a client. Some days, you can spend time on a proposal for new business, some time on developing a new product or service, and some time on performing general research on a specific issue. All of these activities are important to continued success, but they hurt you because none of them are chargeable to a specific client. In other words, the firm isn't getting paid for this work. While the firm values this non-chargeable work, it doesn't want you doing too much of it – it wants you out there making money for the firm. So when you find yourself doing this stuff, your chargeability goes down and your performance numbers suffer, which can hurt your reviews, your paycheck and ultimately your future at the firm. However, you can't err on the other side either – you bill too many hours to your clients and you run the risk of going over budget and having the client give you the third degree on why the job is taking you so long. It can be pretty stressful."

Celebrity Accountants

While accountants usually stick to the finance field, a number of famous people have been through accounting training and have become Certified Public Accountants.

- Nike CEO Phil Knight and Home Depot co-founder Arthur Blank are CPAs.

- Author John Grisham received his undergraduate degree in accounting.

- Former Texas Rangers manager Kevin Kennedy, a CPA, did his players' tax returns to make extra money when he managed in the minor leagues.

- Track sensation and current Villanova University track and field coach Marcus O'Sullivan passed the CPA exam.

- Nearly 1,400 of the FBI's special agents are accountants. In fact, the No. 3 man at the FBI, Assistant FBI Director Thomas Pickard, is a CPA.

- Ray Wersching, the ex-San Francisco 49er place kicker who holds the record for most career field goals in the Super Bowl, was a CPA during the off-season.

Source: New Jersey Society of CPAs

Types of Accounting

Accounting can be broadly divided into two categories: financial accounting and management accounting.

Financial Accounting: Financial accounting is a particular field of accounting that addresses the needs of decision makers outside a company or organization. These decision makers may include credit and equity investors, suppliers, lenders, government agencies and regulatory bodies, special interest groups, labor unions, consumer groups and the general public.

Financial accounting tends to be driven by rules, issued by the Securities and Exchange Commission (SEC), the Financial Accounting Standards Board (FASB) and the International Accounting Standards Committee (IASC).

The objectives of financial reporting are to provide information that is:

(1) Useful to those making investment and credit decisions who have a reasonable understanding of business and economic activities;

(2) Helpful to present and potential investors and creditors and other users in assessing the amount, timing and uncertainty of future cash flows; and

(3) About economic resources, the claims to those resources and the changes in them.

While these objectives are aimed at satisfying the equity and credit investors (whom the FASB considers to be the primary users of financial statements), they are likely to be useful to all other user groups.

Different financial statement users have both coinciding and conflicting needs for the various statements. In general, equity investors are concerned with a company's long-term earnings and growth, as well as its ability to offer returns via dividends and stock price appreciation. Equity investors bear the company's largest and most volatile risk, and thus require comprehensive analyses that offer the highest level of scrutiny. On the other hand, credit investors, such as banks and other lenders, place more specific emphasis on the company's ability to assure the repayment of their investment (via interest payments and the return of principal at maturity).

The financial accounting process culminates in the preparation of financial reports relative to the enterprise as a whole that help answer the following questions about a firm's financial success: What is the financial position of the firm on a given day? How well did the firm do during a given period?

To answer these questions, and to satisfy the fiduciary reporting responsibility of management, accountants prepare a single set of general-purpose financial statements that are expected to fairly, clearly, and completely present the economic facts of the operations of the enterprise. In preparing financial statements, accountants are confronted with the potential dangers of bias, misinterpretation, inexactness and ambiguity.

The four primary financial statements are the Balance Sheet, Income Statement, Statement of Retained Earnings and Statement of Cash Flows. (See p. 19 for an explanation of these statements.)

Management Accounting: As opposed to financial accounting, management accounting serves internal management decision makers at a company or organization. Examples of these managers would include top executives at corporations, college deans and hospital administrators.

Management accounting involves the identification, measurement, accumulation, analysis, preparation, and communication of financial information that is then used by managers to plot strategy and make decisions.

Management accountants may make recommendations on business strategy, resource allocation, cost efficiencies and operations to improve financial performance. The Chief Financial Officer (CFO) position can be considered the highest management accounting position.

A History of Accounting

As old as civilization itself

Accounting is nearly as old as civilization itself. Early accounting practitioners played pivotal roles in the development of writing (the first known instances of writing are inventory records in the Near East) and the creation of money and banking systems. By making business more efficient (and thus freeing up more capital for the endowment of the arts), accounting also played a pivotal role in the flourishing of the Italian Renaissance.

Accounting was firmly established as a distinct profession in 19th century Great Britain during the Industrial Revolution. The rapid rise of manufacturing innovation increased entrepreneurs' concerns over operating costs, leading to the development of rudimentary cost accounting systems. With bankruptcy rates high, such systems helped firms identify and reduce costs and more quickly respond to economic downturns. The advancements also necessitated an increase in formal business regulation and taxation, setting the stage for the establishment of the first professional accounting firms in London by William Deloitte (1845), Samuel Price and Edwin Waterhouse (1849), William Cooper (1854), William Peat (1867), and George Touch. These firms soon established offices in America after the turn of the century (along with the Ernst brothers, Charles Haskins, William Lybrand, Adam and Edward Ross, Elijah Sells, Arthur Young and Arthur Andersen) to oversee investments in America's growing industries. (These early firms still exist as what are called the "Big Four" accounting firms.)

Accounting in the U.S.

Before 1900, the U.S. economy required a relatively unsophisticated type of accounting function; the accounting profession per se was virtually nonexistent. In the 1800s and before, single ownership was the dominant form of business organization in the U.S. Accounting reports for these businesses emphasized solvency and liquidity and were limited to internal use and scrutiny by banks and other lending institutions. Audits were a minor aspect of an accountant's practice; when they were performed, they were viewed as a way to make managers and directors accountable to absentee stockholders for the stewardship of assets.

From 1900 to 1929, the growth of large corporations and the increasing investment and speculation in the stocks of these corporations created the phenomenon of absentee ownership — businesses were owned in large part by outside investors, as opposed to families who directly managed and owned businesses. This in turn created a demand for greater disclosure and a change from the concern with solvency to a concern with income-producing ability. A constitutional amendment in 1913 authorizing the federal government to impose an income tax on businesses and individuals intensified the emphasis on income measurement. As a result of the stock market crash of 1929, the Great Depression and widespread dissatisfaction with the integrity and completeness of available accounting reports, the federal government, the stock exchanges and the accounting profession all made efforts to improve accounting. Since that time, the environmental influences on the development of accounting principles have been primarily institutional or organizational.

Government regulation

The Great Depression, which resulted in the widespread collapse of businesses and the securities market, was the impetus for government intervention and regulation of business. This intervention involved a good deal of attention to financial statements and accounting standards. A direct result was the creation of the Securities and Exchange Commission (SEC) as an independent regulatory agency of the U.S. government to administer the Securities Act of 1933, the Securities Exchange Act of 1934 and several other related pieces of legislation. Companies that issue securities to the public or are listed on stock exchanges are required to file annual audited financial statements with the SEC. In addition, the SEC was given broad powers to prescribe, in whatever detail it desires, the accounting practices and standards to be employed by companies that fall within its jurisdiction.

Until the 1960s, the SEC acted with remarkable restraint in the area of developing accounting standards. Generally, it relied on a trade organization called the American Institute of Certified Public Accountants (AICPA) to regulate the accounting profession and develop and enforce accounting standards. However, during the era of the beleaguered Accounting Principles Board (from 1959 to 1973), the SEC took a more active interest in the development of accounting standards, pressing for quicker action, specific announcements and eventually for the demise of the APB (after which the Financial Accounting Standards Board was established). Now, the FASB establishes the pronouncement of a common set of standards and procedures called Generally Accepted Accounting Principles (GAAP).

Today, the SEC interacts with the FASB as both a supporter and a prodder. Because it confronts the financial accounting and reporting practices of U.S. businesses, the SEC frequently identifies emerging problems for the FASB to address.

Financial Regulation and the U.S. Financial Reporting System

The Securities and Exchange Commission: In the United States, the Securities and Exchange Commission (SEC) governs the form and content of financial statements. Although the SEC has delegated much of this responsibility to the Financial Accounting Standards Board (discussed later), it frequently adds its own requirements and functions as an enforcement mechanism for standards promulgated in the private sector. For example, the SEC-mandated Management Discussion and Analysis (MD&A) provides helpful information regarding past operating results and current financial position. In many cases, SEC-required disclosures preceded FASB action.

Audited financial statements, related footnotes and supplementary data are presented in both annual reports sent to stockholders and those filed with the SEC. These filings often contain other valuable information not presented in stockholder reports. Quarterly financial reports and SEC 10-Q filings, both of which contain abbreviated financial statements, may be reviewed by auditors but are rarely audited.

The American Institute of Certified Public Accountants: The American Institute of Certified Public Accountants (AICPA) is the national professional organization of certified public accountants (CPAs). The AICPA's efforts have been central to the development of GAAP in the United States. Over the years it has formed, with various levels of success, a number of special committees whose purposes were to determine, among other things, proper accounting principles.

After the Depression, the AICPA formed the Committee on Accounting Procedure (CAP), the institute's first attempt to address modern accounting issues. From 1939 to 1959, CAP issued 51 Accounting Research Bulletins dealing with a variety of accounting problems. Despite all of CAP's successes, it did not generate the necessary structured set of accounting principles. Thus, the AICPA formed the Accounting Principles Board (APB) in 1959.

The APB was formed to develop a well-defined conceptual framework that would set forth a written set of accounting principles, determine appropriate accounting practices and address inconsistencies in current accounting practice. From inception to its dissolution in 1973, the board issued 31 APB Opinions. However, while these opinions succeeded in solidifying accounting practice to some degree, the APB ultimately failed due to charges of a lack of productivity, a failure to act quickly in correcting abuses, a strong level of dissention from CPA firms and occasional government intervention. Thus, in 1973, the Financial Accounting Standards Board was formed.

The Financial Accounting Standards Board: The Financial Accounting Standards Board (FASB) is a nongovernmental body with seven full-time members that sets accounting standards for all companies issuing audited financial statements. FASB pronouncements are considered authoritative and immediately become part of GAAP, the governing framework for financial reporting in the United States.

Financial Statements

The four basic financial statements are: the Balance Sheet, the Income Statement, the Statement of Retained Earnings and the Statement of Cash Flows (the names of the statements are capitalized). These statements, along with additional data and analysis, are included in annual reports filed by public companies. We'll examine these statements briefly; prospective accountants should encounter and master these statements early in their accounting education.

The Balance Sheet

The Balance Sheet is a snapshot of a company's financial position at a given point in time. It is comprised of three parts: assets, liabilities and equity.

- **Assets** are the economic resources of a company. They are tangible resources a company uses to operate its business and include Cash, Inventory and Equipment (accounts in financial statements are capitalized).

- **Liabilities** are the company's debts. Liabilities are the claim that creditors have on a company's resources.

- **Equity** is the net worth of a company. It represents the claims a company's shareholders have on its resources.

This is the basic format of a Balance Sheet:

Media Entertainment, Inc
Balance Sheet
(December 31, 2005)

Assets		Liabilities	
Cash	203,000	Accounts Payable	7,000
Accounts Receivable	26,000		
Building	19,000	**Equity**	
		Common Stock	10,000
		Retained Earnings	231,000
Total Assets	248,000	**Total Liabilities & Equity**	248,000

The Income Statement

The Income Statement represents the results of a company's business over a specific time period (e.g., one year, one quarter, etc.) and includes Revenues, Expenses and Net Income.

- **Revenue** is the income that results from a company's sale of its goods or services and is recorded when it is earned.

- **Expenses** are the costs incurred by a company in a given time period to generate the revenues earned during that same period of time.

- **Net Income** is the difference between revenues and expenses.

For example, in order for a manufacturer to produce a product it must buy the materials necessary to make that product and pay the people who make and sell that product. Recording the revenue and expenses in the proper time period is a key accounting principle; abusing or ignoring this principle has landed many companies in hot water. Some companies have been known to sign a contract for a sale that won't take place for some time (months or even years in the future). Companies looking to "cook the books" (misleadingly manipulate the numbers), will try to find creative ways to record that revenue for the current quarter or fiscal year in order to make current results and, by extension, the company's operations and management, look artificially good. This practice can be dangerous. For one thing, the company often doesn't collect any money until the actual transaction takes place. Based on the fudged numbers, a company's shareholders, creditors and suppliers may think the firm has more cash than it actually does, which can prove disastrous if a company has to make a payment. Additionally, sales booked in advance can be canceled, meaning the company will never collect the revenue it already reported.

This is how a basic Income Statement looks:

Media Entertainment, Inc
Income Statement
(For the year ended December 31, 2005)

Revenues		
Services Billed		100,000
Expenses		
Salaries and Wages	(33,000)	
Rent Expense	(17,000)	
Utilities Expense	(7,000)	(57,000)
Net Income		43,000

The Statement of Retained Earnings

The Statement of Retained Earnings is a reconciliation of the Retained Earnings account from the beginning of the year. When a company announces income or declares dividends, this information is reflected in the Statement of Retained Earnings. Net income increases the Retained Earnings account. Net losses and dividend payments decrease Retained Earnings. The Statement of Retained Earnings doesn't provide any information that isn't available in other financial statements. It's meant to be a quick analysis of what management is doing with a company's earnings.

This is a sample Statement of Retained Earnings:

Media Entertainment, Inc
Statement of Retained Earnings
(For the year ended December 31, 2005)

Retained Earnings, January 1, 2005	$200,000
Plus: Net income for the year	43,000
	243,000
Less: Dividends declared	(12,000)
Retained Earnings, December 31, 2005	$ 231,000

The Statement of Cash Flows

The Statement of Cash Flows presents a detailed picture of all cash inflows and outflows during a given period. It's divided into three categories.

- **Cash flows from operating activities** includes the cash effects from transactions involved in calculating net income.

- **Cash flows from investing activities** is cash from non-operating activities. This involves items classified as assets on the Balance Sheet, such as the purchase or sale of equipment or investments.

- **Cash flows from financing activities** includes items identified as liabilities and equity on the Balance Sheet, such as the payment of dividends or paying off debts.

This is the basic format of a Statement of Cash Flows:

Media Entertainment, Inc
Statement of Cash Flows
(For the year ended December 31, 2005)

Cash flows provided from operating activities		
Net Income		33,000
Depreciation Expense		10,000
Increase in Accounts Receivable	(26,000)	
Increase in Accounts Payable	7,000	(19,000)
Net cash provided by operating activities		24,000
Cash flows provided from investing activities		
Purchase of Building	(19,000)	
Sale of Long-Term Investment	35,000	
Net cash provided by investing activities		16,000
Cash flows provided from financing activities		
Payment of Dividends	(12,000)	
Issuance of Common Stock	10,000	
Net cash provided by financing activities		(2,000)
Net increase (decrease) in cash		38,000
Cash at the beginning of the year		165,000
Cash at the end of the year		203,000

Industry Trends and Outlook

The Enron effect

The sudden collapse in late 2001 of Houston, Texas-based energy company Enron had a profound effect on the accounting industry. Enron engaged in accounting practices designed to hide the true liabilities of the company-accounting practices that were approved by its auditor, Arthur Andersen. Chicago, Ill.-based Arthur Anderson, a pioneer in the industry, was convicted on a federal obstruction of justice charge for destroying evidence related to its Enron engagement, eliminating the firm as a major player in the auditing industry. The subsequent collapse of telecom giant WorldCom, also audited by Andersen, in late 2002, only underscored this conclusion. But the Enron scandal had other effects, including increased scrutiny on the accounting and professional services industry.

The unfortunate results of the Enron affair are dramatic and far-reaching: one of the largest bankruptcies in U.S. history, $32 billion lost in market capitalization, $1 billion lost in employee retirement accounts, and the first-ever felony conviction of a public accounting firm. Furthermore, the scandal, along with other recent, high-profile audit failures at companies from Waste Management and Cendant to more recent scandals involving Italian dairy company Parmalat, to SEC settlements involving companies such as Bristol-Myers Squibb and Qwest, to current investigations into mortgage investment giant Fannie Mae, has damaged the integrity and credibility of the public accounting profession in the eyes of senior executives and the public at large. And it's not just Arthur Andersen that has suffered in light of these developments; three of the Big Four accounting firms have endured similar investigations by the SEC in the past couple of years, with numerous questionable tactics being descried by authorities. KPMG was recently charged with unprofessional conduct in a scandal involving audits of Gemstar, and agreed to pay $10 million in fines. PricewaterhouseCoopers paid $5 million to the SEC in 2002, formerly the largest fine for any infractions. Ernst & Young is currently under investigation for alleged violations.

How will these events affect the future of the accounting profession? A number of reforms have been proposed, including: the creation of a private sector oversight board independent of public accountants to monitor audit quality and enforce auditor discipline; the mandate of a timed rotation of auditors; the implementation of limits on auditor moves to client positions; reform of audit committees; and a reassessment of certain accounting rules.

The most significant change thus far has come in the form of the Sarbanes-Oxley act of 2002, which established an expansive set of rules meant to prevent the kind of accounting fraud evidenced at places like Enron and Tyco. And these kinds of reforms have even come into play at the academic level, as colleges and other accounting programs have begun to address the ethical aspect of the profession throughout their curriculum.

No more consulting?

Chief among the reforms is the ban on consulting services. In recent years, the large professional services firms have been divesting their management consulting practices, a trend underscored by then volatile, highly publicized split between Arthur Andersen and Andersen Consulting (now known as Accenture) in 2000. Arguably, these divestitures were more a result of internal revenue-sharing disputes between auditors and consultants (consulting work generally commands significantly higher margins than audit work) and attempts to realize the value of such consulting practices via initial public offerings than a desire to secure greater auditor independence. But critics of the industry have long been skeptical about accounting firms' financial dependence on their consulting arms, pointing out the inherent difficulty in auditors' maintaining any sense of objectivity while their firms are so beholden to clients for consulting revenue. In early 2002, PricewaterhouseCoopers and Deloitte Touche Tohmatsu, the last professional services firms to offer management consulting as part of their primary service portfolios, agreed to split off the consulting practices to appease those who fretted about the potential conflicts of interest.

While there formerly was no general proscription by either the SEC or the AICPA against performing non-auditing services for audit clients, Congressional action has changed this. A number of congressional subcommittees have looked at the issue of auditor independence, and there already is legislation that limits auditing firms from providing both audit and consulting services to the same client. In fact, a number of states are considering legislation which will ban this practice entirely going forward. The Sarbanes-Oxley Act (or Sarbox), along with the PCAOB (Public Company Accounting Oversight Board) has already restricted the nonauditing services that public accountants (which include the Big Four) can provide to clients; if they audit a client's financial statements, the same firm is not allowed to offer advice in the areas of human resources, technology, investment banking, or legal matters, although accountants may still advise on tax issues. Accountants may still advise other clients in these areas, or may give advice within their own firm. The effects of this ban can still vary, depending on the specific definition of consulting services, but as legislation continues to evolve, there are sure to be further changes down the road.

Besides shareholders and employees, the Enron scandal also took as a victim one of the most prominent firms in the accounting profession. After it was revealed that Arthur Andersen approved Enron's complicated and illegal offshore partnerships, government investigators began looking at Andersen. The firm admitted in early 2002 that it shredded documents related to Enron, even after the government obtained a subpoena for the information. The Justice Department began seeking an indictment of Andersen, wrecking the firm's reputation. Clients were defecting in droves, and staff and partners domestically and worldwide were leaving. In an 11th-hour bid to save the firm, former Fed chairman Paul Volcker outlined a plan to create a seven-member management board that would, among other things, divest Andersen of its consulting businesses and make it the model for proper accounting and audit procedure. Unfortunately, Volcker's plan was contingent upon an improbable confluence of events: the Justice Department dropping its investigation, shareholders settling lawsuits and partners committing themselves to stay and salvage the firm. None of those things happened, and the firm hoped to salvage itself through a merger with a competitor. Again, no luck. Arthur Andersen was tried for obstruction of justice in federal court; in June 2002, in a rare event, a major corporation was found guilty of a felony in a jury trial. Andersen surrendered its audit license in August 2002, leaving a hole in the industry to be filled by the Big Four (nee Big Five) and smaller audit firms. And the Big Four have certainly prospered at the hands of Andersen's demise-by mid-fall 2002, Ernst & Young had picked up more than 200 ex-Andersen clients, while the other Big Four firms had picked up in excess of 100 each. And that doesn't even account for the fact that in some cases, these firms have acquired entire formerly Andersen offices; in some cases, teams of former Andersen accountants have migrated to these other firms, bringing rosters of clients with them.

Dwindling numbers

Even before Enron, the accounting profession witnessed a significant decrease in new membership. According to the AICPA, the number of students graduating with accounting degrees fell 23 percent between 1996 and 2000, as students turned increasingly to careers in finance, information technology, and other business disciplines. The taint from the scandal could further deter students from pursuing an accounting career. However, the increased emphasis on the quality of accounting and auditing could make the profession more attractive to students seeking challenging, meaningful

Visit the Vault Finance Career Channel at **www.vault.com/finance** — with insider firm profiles, message boards, the Vault Finance Job Board and more.

VAULT CAREER LIBRARY   25

assignments and high levels of responsibility. However, the increased emphasis on the quality of accounting and auditing could make the profession more attractive to students seeking challenging, meaningful assignments and high levels of responsibility. And a number of accounting programs are now incorporating increased ethics-related material into their curriculum, and the Big Four, the American Accounting Association, the AICPA, and the Institute of Management Accountants have all joined universities to help develop this aspect of curricula. Ethics-related changes to the CPA exam may follow.

And ultimately, according to the Bureau of Labor Statistics, accounting and accounting-related jobs are forecasted to grow on average through 2010. And aside from an increase in the number of businesses who will need auditing services, the changing financial laws and regulations and the increased scrutiny of company finances in today's culture will only power the drive the growth of accountants and auditors.

Technology and globalization

The Big Four firms in particular are increasingly stewards in technological advancement, and are among the most shrewd and aggressive of all businesses in their embrace of intranets, extranets and e-commerce technology. In addition, there is a movement throughout the field towards adoption of international accounting rules. Though this issue is still evolving, there is no question that international accounting organizations, such as the International Federation of Accountants (IFAC) and the International Accounting Standards Committee (IASC), will wield more influence in the future.

Accounting Services

CHAPTER 2

The term "accounting firm" might now actually be somewhat misleading. Traditional accounting organizations have developed a number of services beyond their traditional audit and tax functions (discussed below). Indeed, the Big Four and the larger second-tier organizations have long since discarded this designation for the more comprehensive "professional services firm" appellation.

However, it should be noted that the provision of many of these services by traditional accounting firms has come under increased scrutiny for potential conflicts of interest as a result of the Enron collapse. In particular, accounting firms are increasingly under pressure to divorce their management consulting services (see "Industry Trends and Outlook" in the previous chapter) from their accounting services.

In this chapter, we break down the services commonly offered by the larger accounting firms, although the list below should not be considered an exhaustive one. Also, be aware that the number and types of services that can be offered by accounting firms can change as quickly as the overall business climate.

Audit, assurance and advisory

The most basic functions of CPA (short for Certified Public Accountant, the professional designation for accountants) firms are accounting and auditing, which consist primarily of performing independent audits of the financial statements issued by companies. A company is a client of its accounting firm — it pays the accounting firm to audit its financial statements. The accounting firm's audit signals that an independent authority attests to their validity. In addition, a number of audit-related services are offered, either as part of the audit engagement or as a separate engagement. Among those services are:

- Recommending improvements on internal controls, operating efficiencies and profitability to management

- Acquisition audits (financial analysis or "due diligence" on a company the client is considering acquiring)

- Validating financial and non-financial data for internal and external review

- Confirming that the client is in compliance with debt agreements

Taxation

The provision of tax services has developed far beyond the mundane preparation of tax returns. Generally, these services focus on the creation of strategies to minimize tax liability (reduce the amount of tax payments) and comply with local, federal and international law. Specific tax services now cover a wide range of issues:

- Accounting for taxes on financial statements
- The preparation of federal, state and local tax returns
- Advisory on multi-state and international taxation issues
- Consultation on mergers and acquisitions to minimize taxes
- Structuring operations to leverage tax opportunities
- Reviewing tax returns for compliance with tax laws
- Personal wealth and estate planning for individuals

A firm's tax practice often includes special service groups that address specific, complex tax issues. For example, some accounting firms maintain groups that monitor new tax laws, regulations, rulings, cases and other developments within the tax regulatory environment and communicate this knowledge to the rest of the firm. Often, these practices are located in Washington, D.C., and employ attorneys and engineers to advise on the tax aspects of complex transactions.

Corporate finance and risk management services

This area covers a broad range of services designed to assess and manage organizational risk from strategic, tactical and financial perspectives. These include:

- Internal controls review and transformation
- Internal audit outsourcing (i.e., handling audit functions for clients)
- Operations benchmarking and advisory services (reviewing the client's operations and comparing it to competitors)
- E-business security consulting

Financial risk management services include the quantitative assessment of the financial impacts of business risk and the creation of highly structured financing strategies composed of risk management products (e.g., options, futures, swaps) to address such risks.

Transaction services

This area employs audit and tax professionals to maximize the returns on merger, acquisition and divestiture transactions, analyzing each stage of the transaction process for both the buy-side and the sell-side to realize full value. These services may include:

• Financial and tax due diligence

• Transaction structuring

• Capital raising assistance

Business process outsourcing

CPA firms often have both the expertise and size to assume the operation of many of the non-critical functions of their clients. Firms outsource such services in order to focus resources on their core functions and to rationalize non-operating costs. The functions commonly outsourced to CPA firms include finance and accounting, enterprise resource planning systems, human resources, training and education and information technology.

Litigation consulting

The larger CPA firms offer financial, economic and statistical services to parties involved in litigation, arbitrations, mediations and other forms of dispute resolution processes. These services may include: forensic accounting and investigation; management, valuation and defense of intellectual property; analyses related to antitrust situations; securities litigation services; asset tracing and recovery services; insurance litigation and fraud detection; and computer/information technology forensics.

Environmental accounting

As businesses have increased their awareness of environmental issues, CPAs have been getting involved in everything from environmental compliance audits and systems and procedures audits to handling claims and disputes. Companies in the utilities, manufacturing and chemical production areas have increasingly turned to CPAs to set up preventative systems to ensure compliance and avoid future claims or disputes, or to provide assistance once legal implications have arisen.

Visit the Vault Finance Career Channel at **www.vault.com/finance** — with
insider firm profiles, message boards, the Vault Finance Job Board and more.

VAULT CAREER LIBRARY   **29**

Personal financial planning

CPAs provide assistance to individuals in identifying financial objectives and counseling on the risk, liquidity, management and tax characteristics of investments. These services include helping clients better manage their money through debt reduction and expense control, developing investment strategies and asset allocation plans, tax consulting, insurance analysis and planning, retirement and estate and gift tax planning.

Management consulting

Management consulting addresses an infinite array of issues related to the overall performance and direction of a firm's business. These services include systems integration, business strategy, e-commerce and technology consulting and human resources.

Breakdown of Accounting Careers

CHAPTER 3

Types of Accountants

Just as there are types of accounting, there are also types of accountants. While there are many ways to classify accountants, the most common division is between public and private accountants.

Public accountants mainly deal with financial accounting (the preparation of financial statements for external parties such as investors). Private accountants deal with both financial and management accounting.

Public accountants

Public accountants receive a fee for services provided to individuals, businesses and governments. Public accounting firms vary greatly in size and the type of services provided. Most public accounting firms provide some combination of auditing, tax and management consulting services. Small firms mainly provide tax or bookkeeping services for smaller companies and organizations that do not have internal accounting departments. Larger firms usually provide these services to firms that have internal accounting departments. Because all public companies are required to have yearly audits, the large public accounting firms are extremely important for fulfilling this requirement.

The four largest accounting firms are known as the "Big Four," and are among the most well-known organizations throughout the world. (Previously, it was the Big Eight, which became the Big Six and then the Big Five when PriceWaterhouse and Coopers & Lybrand merged to form PricewaterhouseCoopers. Because of the collapse of Arthur Andersen, we're now down to the Big Four. See p. 10 for basic information on the Big Four.) The Big Four is made up of:

- Deloitte & Touche
- Ernst & Young
- KPMG
- PricewaterhouseCoopers

Visit the Vault Finance Career Channel at www.vault.com/finance — with insider firm profiles, message boards, the Vault Finance Job Board and more.

VAULT CAREER LIBRARY

31

Many students pursuing accounting careers aim to start their careers at one of the Big Four firms. The Big Four have offices throughout the United States, as well as in many other countries. These firms recruit at a majority of the top schools throughout the world.

In addition to the Big Four, there are thousands of other accounting firms ranging from small proprietorships to large international partnerships. The difference between these firms and the Big Four is size, often measured in terms of billings. The Big Four have billings in excess of $1 billion a year. A large majority (97 percent) of companies listed on the New York Stock Exchange are clients of the Big Four.

Regional accounting firms represent clients that do most of their business within the U.S., although they may also have a few international clients. The largest regional firms can be thought of as somewhat smaller versions of the Big Four. And as the category name suggests, these practices tend to be stronger in certain regions. If you're considering working for a regional public accounting firm, be sure to research the quality of the firm's practice in your area. The large regional players include Grant Thornton, BDO Seidman, and Jackson Hewitt.

Local accounting firms operate in a small number of cities and tend to focus on small businesses and individuals. These organizations conduct more tax and tax planning engagements and traditionally handle more of the bookkeeping responsibilities for their clients.

While most people start their careers at a public accounting firm, many gain valuable experience in public accounting and switch to the private sector after two years (or however long it takes them to get certified as a CPA). Accountants with public accounting experience are well positioned to take financial officer positions at corporations, government agencies or non-profits.

Private accountants

Private accountants work for businesses, the government or non-profit agencies.

Corporations – Most corporations have an internal accounting group that prepares the financial information (both tax and audit) for the public accountants, tracks company performance for internal evaluation and works with management on issues related to acquisitions, international transactions and any other operational issues that arise in the running of the company.

Within corporations, there are several roles that an accountant can take on. These include, but are not limited to the following:

- **Internal auditors** perform financial accounting tasks within an organization. Typically, these employees will perform audits of specific divisions or operational units of a company.

- **Management accountants** can work in several different areas of a corporation. On the finance side, accountants can work in the financial planning and analysis or treasurer's group, analyzing potential acquisitions and making funding decisions for the company. On the accounting side, there are opportunities within the accounting group to handle tax issues and to work with external auditors to prepare financial statements such as SEC filings. Additionally, on the accounting side, opportunities exist to work within specific divisions to track costs and analyze operational performance.

Government agencies – Government accountants can work at the federal, state or local level. Many government organizations have large accounting departments to analyze the performance and allocation of their funds. The Department of Defense (DOD), the General Accounting Office (GAO), the Internal Revenue Service (IRS) and the Securities and Exchange Commission (SEC) typically hire large numbers of accountants for services and evaluations within the organization. Accountants at the IRS typically review individual and corporate tax returns. The SEC hires experienced accountants to evaluate filings made by public companies. These accountants ensure that firms are complying with SEC regulations.

Non-profit organizations – Accounting for non-profits is very similar to for-profit accounting; they both follow Generally Accepted Accounting Principles (GAAP). In addition to understanding GAAP, non-profit accountants must also understand the FASB standards written specifically for these organizations as well as the tax regulations specific to those organizations. (For example, non-profit organizations are typically exempt from federal taxation.)

The accounting groups in these organizations are typically smaller than those in for-profit companies, so an employee may be responsible for more than one area of accounting (e.g., both financial statements and tax issues).

Visit the Vault Finance Career Channel at **www.vault.com/finance** — with
insider firm profiles, message boards, the Vault Finance Job Board and more.

V∧ULT CAREER LIBRARY   **33**

Public or Private?

According to many college professors and career services counselors, most college students interested in accounting should try to start their careers in public accounting. This route carries a number of benefits, including higher salaries, more interesting and diverse work, exposure to many different industries and the ability to fulfill a requirement for certification (see "The CPA" chapter, which starts on p. 51).

One senior manager at a Big Four firm captures the general opinion of the majority of people we spoke with: "For someone just out of college, public accounting is really the only way to go," he says. "You gain experience and get up the learning curve much more quickly. A public accountant will perform three or four audits of entire companies in a year, whereas a private accountant could be stuck monitoring cash ledgers – one account – for a year. Even in the long term, there are benefits. You have more control over your career progression. In private, you'll often see highly productive and talented individuals mired in their jobs or limited to lateral career moves because they have to wait for the people above them to retire or otherwise leave the company. Public accounting is much more of a meritocracy – you'll advance as fast and as high as you want to."

However, public accounting life is not for everyone. Private accountants generally don't travel nearly as much as public accountants, and their work schedules are much more stable – they rarely have to pack a briefcase and go to a client at a moment's notice. Private accountants also do not have to deal with the chargeability issue (the pressure on public accountants to work on billable projects as much of the time as possible). Finally, they are not required to get their CPA and thus do not have to deal with the rigors of fulfilling the grueling certification requirements (discussed further on p. 53).

GETTING HIRED

Competition on the Street – and beyond – is heating up. With the finance job market tightening, you need to be your best.

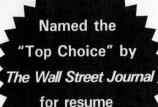

Hiring Process
and Interviews

There are currently more than 46,000 public accounting firms, ranging in size from local practices to the Big Four and other international practices. By all accounts, there should be no shortage of opportunities in accounting in the near future. The U.S. Bureau of Labor Statistics expects accounting employment to grow at least as fast as the average for all U.S. occupations through the year 2006. The increasing complexity and number of business transactions require the specialized knowledge and skills of more accountants and auditors to analyze and interpret data.

However, the competition for these spots will intensify as the roles of accountants transform. As accounting software takes over more and more of the old "bean counting," accountants will increasingly be asked to provide more value-added service and to become more helpful as business strategists. Thus, aspiring accountants must have a broader range of skills that includes communications, analytical and other general management skills, in addition to technical accounting knowledge.

How Do I Get a Job?

There are several ways to break into the field of accounting. The most straightforward is through on-campus recruiting. The others include making contacts and identifying opportunities through the Internet or friends and family.

Internships at the Big Four

The easiest way to get a full-time job at one of the Big Four accounting firms is through the internship process. Each of the public accounting firms hires a large class of interns from all of the top schools and from many regional schools each year. A majority of these interns will receive full-time offers at their internship firms.

If you want a job at one of the Big Four firms, remember you have only four chances to get a job. These opportunities are each precious, so prepare thoroughly ahead of time. Know all the answers to the typical questions (discussed later in this chapter). No matter what your goal is, in order to succeed in getting a good internship, you need to be well prepared for all of your interviews.

For internship interviews, most of the questions will be "behavioral" (rather than technical questions about accounting). But you should be prepared for some of the basic technical questions. Competition is fierce – know why you want to work in accounting, why at that specific firm and why they should hire you. These are some of the basic questions. There are more questions listed in the interview section.

The value of summer internships

Summer internships are valuable because they offer the student a chance to get a sense of their early job responsibilities. Usually, summer interns perform work similar to work done by full-time employees in their first year of employment. Another possibility is to consider taking a semester off from classes to pursue an internship with a firm during their "busy season," typically the period between January and April. This can result in credit toward an accounting degree as well as a large lead in climbing the experience curve. Many public accountants claim they learn more during this period than any other time during the year. Stated one former senior accountant at a large firm, "Learning definitely comes in waves within this industry. Those particular three months represent a tidal wave of learning and work."

Other internships

If your goal is to end up full-time at one of the Big Four, but don't land an internship at one of the them, don't lose hope — you can still get a full-time position. The next step is to make sure that you obtain an internship in a related position.

For instance, you can work at a smaller public accounting firm, a government institution or in an accounting role within the corporate finance or accounting departments of a large corporation. Even relevant work at a small company can help. "In my sophomore year in college," says one senior tax accountant at a Big Four firm, "I was the accountant for a small, local heating and air conditioning company. I pretty much handled their little general ledger and prepared their federal and state tax returns, nothing too complicated. Later, when I was interviewing with the Big Four, they were very interested in my small company experience, even though I had since worked for a large investment bank and had a summer internship at one of the Big Four."

Full-time positions

Because most of the Big Four firms hire a significant portion of their full-time accountants from the internship class, competition is tough for those seeking to land a full-time position without an internship. Prepare well. Be able to explain why your internship has prepared you for a full-time position at one of the Big Four. Whatever your goal is, if you work hard and prepare well, you can succeed.

Interviews will be mostly behavioral, designed to assess how you have handled, or would handle, certain situations relevant to the profession. However, firms will expect you to be more proficient with the technical aspects of accounting than they will be during the internship recruiting process. You will have some basic technical questions. The companies are not necessarily looking for the one correct answer, they want to know your thought process.

If you do not begin your career in public accounting, you can still get into the profession later on. Individuals with valuable work experience in certain industries are hired directly from their firms to work at all levels within the public accounting firms. Depending on what type of work you want to do (auditing, tax, etc.), focus your resume on the type of work that is relevant to those jobs. This will make the transition to public accounting significantly easier.

Outside the Big Four public accounting firms

So what about companies other than the Big Four? On-campus recruiting focuses on the Big Four and large corporations for a few reasons. From a professional development standpoint, these employers tend to have well-established training programs that mitigate a college graduate's lack of experience and give new hires the opportunity to quickly get up the learning curve. Smaller firms often do not have the ability to devote large resources to entry-level training. Furthermore, according to *New Accountant*, many professors feel that placing students in these high profile positions enhances the perceived quality of an accounting program. Consequently, smaller firms faced with this situation often limit their recruiting efforts to visiting smaller colleges or to luring experienced accountants away from the Big Four.

However, there are a good number of non-Big Four opportunities available to new college graduates, including positions in private industry and government. According to one campus career counselor, these opportunities, while generally fewer in number, still require the same qualities in their new hires as the Big Four. In some cases, says this counselor, these positions require stronger skills and abilities than the Big Four – since the company does not have the same level of training available at the Big Four, it wants its new hires to come in with the strongest possible credentials.

Some of these job opportunities are available via the same on-campus recruiting processes you would use to seek Big Four positions. Expect their presentations to have a more comparative than informative tone, telling you all the reasons why you should come work for them rather than a Big Four firm. In the view of one recent accounting graduate, these smaller firms' presentations and personnel had a more intimate, "down-to-earth" feel, giving the impression that you would be able to make more of an immediate impact at their smaller firms than at the Big Four.

If you don't find them on campus, you'll have to do a little more legwork. Realize that virtually every company – private or public, profit or non-profit – and government agency has some kind of accounting function. So, the encouraging thing is that virtually every organization in the country might have a position for you. A useful first step is to make a list of companies you'd be interested in based on your own criteria (e.g., industry, geographic location, etc.). Then, do what you can to become familiar with what each company does and the types of opportunities it has available. These days, most corporate web sites have career information, including some sort of job search functionality, and should give you a very specific idea of the kinds of positions available and their requirements. Many will even allow you to apply online.

However, before you cut-and-paste that resume onto the web site, you should exhaust your networking abilities to try to find a reference inside the company you've targeted. Having a professional contact refer you and present your resume is much more effective than an anonymous e-mail or Web posting. According to an accounting recruiter at one large company, resumes presented by current employees are almost always evaluated in short order, while unsolicited e-mails have a higher tendency to sit unread in a bin with dozens of other resumes.

The important thing to remember is that you are selling yourself. On campus, the companies, to some degree, are looking for you and are trying to sell themselves to you. When the tables are turned and you are pursuing the company, you absolutely must be prepared and persistent, and you should also be prepared to face what most likely will be a higher rejection rate. But don't get discouraged. While these jobs might take more work to get, they also could ultimately be more fulfilling.

Educational background

If you're interested in an accounting career, you should choose courses that prepare you for your future profession. (Most states now require accountants to have the equivalent of five years of educational experience covering accounting, business and general knowledge areas in order to be eligible for CPA certification, but you should take these courses regardless of whether you intend to pursue a CPA or not.)

These college-level courses help the aspiring accountant to develop the fundamental competencies, such as strategic thinking, communications and technology proficiency, as well as technical accounting knowledge, that are crucial to the profession. The chart below provides a sample of specific course topics that are most applicable to the accounting profession.

Financial statement analysis	Auditing
Intermediate accounting	Advanced accounting
Corporate finance	Investment accounting
Mergers & acquisitions accounting	Management information systems
Forensic accounting	Environmental accounting
Fraud detection and prevention	Managerial accounting
Cost accounting and control	Not-for-profit and government accounting
Taxation of business entities	Tax strategies for corporations
International tax	Individual tax planning

What do I put on my resume?

Your resume is an opportunity for you to market yourself. The recruiters are not expecting you to have a lot of work experience, but you should point out the skills that are important to accountants. Accountants must be interested in analyzing financial information. All accountants will work in team, interacting throughout their careers with accountants; therefore, communication and interpersonal skills are also extremely important. Computer skills are also important, as working with spreadsheets will be required to analyze financial information.

In addition to analyzing financial information, you will be asked to identify and analyze information processes, evaluate the effectiveness of those procedures and identify recommendations for improving the data processes. In addition, you will be asked to review accounting or tax standards to determine the appropriate accounting, then document and explain the basis for your decisions. As you advance in the firm, you will be required to develop and maintain relationships with clients and sell additional work. You will be asked to deal with difficult clients and issues and determine how to address these issues.

Accountants typically have a strong interest in numbers and analyzing them. Often, you will find that they also have an interest in analyzing process and information flows, identifying improvement opportunities and having the ability to make decisions that will affect the daily operations of clients. Organization and time management are also extremely important, especially during busy season, as you will be expected to work overtime during tax season. You will need to be flexible to accommodate uncertainty, the demands of a heavy workload and potential travel to various client sites. To summarize, the following are the key skills:

- **Analytical skills** – To analyze financial data, identify and explain discrepancies and variations.

- **Teamwork** – To work well with team members and clients to obtain necessary information.

- **Communication** – To interact with clients to discuss issues and obtain information in a professional manner.

- **Organization/time management** – To prioritize and juggle various tasks, and to identify and discuss time constraints.

- **Flexibility** – To adapt to changing clients, schedules and working hours.

As you are preparing your resume, you should ensure that you identify and show these skills as much as possible. You are not expected to talk about each and every aspect of the jobs that you have had, but you should always talk about the experiences that are relevant to your career search.

On-Campus Recruiting

An early start

Many accounting firms recruit on-campus at a number of universities – check with your career services department to determine which firms recruit at your school. If a firm recruits on your campus, make sure that you make contacts at the firm whenever possible.

The recruiting process for undergraduate public accounting hiring begins earlier than for most professions. Usually, students in their final year of college will have their offers in hand by Thanksgiving. The largest firms like to anticipate and fill their personnel needs earlier than many other organizations. This means that accounting students have to be fully prepared for interview season before most of their classmates.

The firms may have a reception prior to the interview date to meet people and form their interview list. If there is a reception, you should attend. Go to the reception dressed appropriately and make at least one or two contacts. Get their business cards and send them a thank-you letter expressing your interest in their firm.

A test of social skills

With an accounting degree from a good school, you have the skills necessary to work in an accounting firm or as an accountant in a corporation. What you have to prove to the interviewer and the firm is that you have the social skills necessary to be successful and relate to their clients. You need to prove that you have good ethical standards and that you're able to make good decisions. The interview process will be discussed in detail later in this chapter.

Regional recruitment

Recruiters work for regional offices and thus recruit for offices in their region. For example, at Virginia Tech, the Big Four firms recruit mostly for the Washington, DC or Virginia offices. If you want to work in an office that is not recruited for directly on your campus, you can request an offer at another office. The recruiters will make a recommendation to the recruiters for the region you desire, but your chances of getting a job will be significantly reduced. It might be a better idea to take an internship at one of the offices a firm is recruiting on your campus for, and trying to secure a transfer after you get your full-time offer.

The Interview Process

There are several steps to the interview process for both internships and full-time positions. The interview process for each school will vary, so make sure to check with your career services department early in the year. If you're really serious about a career in accounting, you want to make sure you don't miss any opportunities to network with existing employees.

The recruiting process for internships and full-time positions is fairly similar. The timing will be a bit different. Internship interviews are conducted in the beginning of spring semester, while full-time interviews occur during the fall. Either way, the recruiting process will begin with a company presentation in the fall. These presentations will give you the opportunity to learn about the various positions available within a company and the locations that they are recruiting for. It is important to attend these presentations to show your interest and to begin networking with the recruiting team. After the presentation, you should try to make at least one or two contacts with the interviewers or the recruiters. In the months that follow, you should contact them with a thank-you letter and with any additional questions you may have. One word of caution: during these presentations, be sure to have your story straight. Anything you say to the recruiters during these presentations may or may not be remembered. Just to be safe, make sure that your later comments remain consistent with those that you initially made at the presentation.

Interview preparation

After the company presentation, it's time to start preparing for the interview. (It's never too early to start preparing for your interviews.) There are several key steps that can help you prepare.

- **Research each firm thoroughly.** Know the firm. Your initial research should allow you to completely understand the opportunities that are available at each firm. You should know the strengths and weaknesses of each firm. Your goal is to impress the interviewer with your knowledge. This will allow you to have a leg up on the other candidates by proving your interest in their specific firm. (For 50-page insider profiles on each of the Big Four firms, get Vault's Accounting Employer Profiles.)

- **Utilize career services.** Start early. Your university will have some services for interview preparation and practice. Take advantage of all of these opportunities – early and often. The career department will have valuable information that can help you prepare for your interview. They have a good idea of what the firms are looking for and what strategies work and don't work.

- **Develop your interview strategy.** Know what skills and strengths of yours you want to emphasize. Keep them in the back of your head at all times and make sure that you are prepared to demonstrate that you have these specific skills and strengths. Prepare your story – be able to tell the recruiter why you picked this university, why public accounting versus private accounting, why tax versus audit.

- **Express your interest.** It is important to continue to express your interest to each of the companies that you would like to interview with. At least one month prior to interviews, you should send the main recruiter a cover letter and resume expressing your interest and requesting a spot on the list of students being interviewed.

- **Prepare answers to sample interview questions.** A later section in this chapter includes some sample interview questions. For internship interviews, expect mostly general questions. The recruiters will want to get an idea of who you are and whether you can function in a team. Are you motivated? Do you have the interpersonal skills that are required to work with clients? Are you willing to learn? These are all going to be important to your recruiter. If you are interviewing for a full-time position, your recruiter will want to understand what you did for your summer internship and they may ask you some technical questions. It is more likely that you will get technical questions for full-time interviews because, theoretically, you would have had an internship in the field of accounting and you will have several accounting classes under your belt.

Finally, the interview

At this point, you have prepared your story and the answers to the typical interview questions. You're ready to wow them with your accounting knowledge. Let's talk about some of the basics. Make sure you are appropriately dressed. Most interviews will require business attire – wear a conservative suit, conservative shoes and little jewelry. Do not wear strong smelling perfumes. Take a portfolio with extra copies of your resume. Show up on time – in fact show up a few minutes early. Give the recruiter a firm handshake. And no matter what, always show poise and confidence throughout the interview. During the interview, the interviewer may try to rattle you. They want to see how you function under pressure. Accountants must show poise and grace in all circumstances. They want to know you have ethics and an active lifestyle. Grades and extracurricular activities will be extremely important. Emphasize your GPA to the interviewer if it's good.

After the interview

Waiting to hear back from the interviewer about whether you made it to second rounds can be gut-wrenching. Each time the phone rings you jump, hoping it's the firm you just interviewed with, calling to ask you back for more interviews or to give you an offer. Everyone goes through this nervousness. Try to go on with your life: continue with your job search, study, hang out with your friends, and prepare for future interviews.

There is one things you can do after the interview to ensure that you've done all you can: send the interviewer a thank-you note. No matter how good or how bad an interview goes, a thank-you note will win you extra points. Make sure the note expresses your continued interest in the firm. Re-emphasize anything that helps you stand out from other interviewees. And a final check – make sure there are no spelling errors.

What now?

A few days after your interview, the firm should contact you with one of two answers: 1) we want you to interview in second rounds, or 2) thanks for your interest, but we can't offer you a job.

If you don't get asked back for second rounds, it's not over. You still have other interviews. Ask the recruiter for feedback and try to fix any problems for your next interview. If you are asked back for second rounds, it's also not over. Second-round interviews can be held either on campus or at the firm's offices. Once again, make sure you're prepared. During these interviews, make sure your answers are always consistent. Ensure that you continue to show interest in the firm. If second rounds are on campus, expect one or two interviews with seniors or managers. If the interviews are on-site, you may have up to six interviews with seniors, managers or partners. Again, make sure you send a thank-you note to each interviewer.

You may receive an offer at second rounds, after second rounds, or you may be asked to come back for third rounds. This will vary by firm.

Visit the Vault Finance Career Channel at **www.vault.com/finance** — with insider firm profiles, message boards, the Vault Finance Job Board and more.

VAULT CAREER LIBRARY   **47**

Sample Interview Questions

Commitment questions: There are no "right" answers to these questions. These questions are meant to assess your commitment to the profession and your career. The interviewer will be looking for a relatively organized thought pattern that indicates that you've really thought about your career goals.

- What are your long-term and short-term goals?
- What do you see yourself doing in five years?
- How do you plan to achieve your goals?
- Why have you chosen this career?
- Why did you select your university or college?
- Why did you choose this field of study?
- What other jobs are you interviewing for?
- What other firms are you interviewing with?
- What are you going to do if you don't get a job in public accounting?
- Why do you want this position with our company?

Maturity questions: These questions are meant to assess your level of maturity, how thoroughly you monitor what you need to improve and how to make those improvements. It would help to know at least two of each.

- What are your strengths and weaknesses?
- What qualifications do you have that will make you successful in your career?
- How do you function under pressure? Give me an example.
- Describe a major problem in your life and how you dealt with it.
- What did you learn from your mistakes?

Motivation questions: Recruiters will want to know what drives you to do your best work and, conversely, what bores you in your work. They'll want to assess how well your motivations and work style fit with their corporate culture.

- What are the most important rewards that you expect in your business career?
- What is more important to you, the money or the type of job?
- What motivates you to put forth the greatest effort?

- How do you determine and evaluate success?

- What are the qualities of a successful manager?

- Why audit and not tax? Why tax and not audit?

- What work environment are you most comfortable in?

- What things are most important to you in your job?

Communications skills questions: These questions are designed to assess your level of preparation for the interview. Interviewers will be looking to see whether you can effectively convey information in a thorough yet concise manner. These questions will also assess how well you think on the run.

- How would you describe yourself?

- How would a friend or a professor describe you?

- How has college prepared you for your chosen career?

- Why should I hire you?

- How can you make a contribution to our company?

- What is your greatest accomplishment?

- Which two or three accomplishments gave you the most satisfaction and why?

- If you were hiring a candidate for this job, what qualities would you look for?

- Are your grades a good indication of your academic achievements?

- Do your grades reflect your abilities?

- What have you learned from your extracurricular activities?

- What do you know about our company?

Technical questions: These questions are designed to test your knowledge of basic accounting and tax. Don't be surprised if you don't get any technical questions at this level, especially if you're interviewing with the Big Four. The expectation is that you can learn the technical stuff – they're more interested in the questions above that test your "fit" with the firm. Nevertheless, it wouldn't hurt to brush up on basic technical questions like these.

- ***What is the matching principle?***

   The recording of expenses in the same time period the related revenues are recognized.

- ## *When do you recognize revenue?*

  When it meets two criteria: 1) it is earned (i.e., goods or services are delivered); and 2) it is realized (i.e., cash or cash claims are received in exchange).

- ## *What does auditing mean to you?*

  Examining transactions and financial statements, in accordance with generally accepted auditing standards, in order to attest to the credulity of those statements.

- ## *What is the current corporate tax rate?*

  35 percent.

- ## *What is the relationship between the income statement and the balance sheet?*

  The income statement is the major link between two balance sheets. Balance sheets show the company's position at given points in time (i.e., year end), whereas the income statement explains the changes that have taken place between those points.

  Net income per the income statement is entered into the balance sheet as retained earnings.

The CPA

Becoming a CPA is no easy task. It demands a higher education commitment than most other career paths. To qualify for certification, you must meet the requirements of the state or jurisdiction where you wish to practice. The state requirements are established by the state board of accountancy and vary from state to state. Because of these variations, first determine where you are planning to practice accounting and then review that state's certification requirements on the web site for the state's CPA society or board of accountancy.

Becoming a certified public accountant entails the successful completion of the following: (a) 150 credit hours of college-level education, which translates to five years of college and graduate level work; (b) achievement of passing grades on all four parts of the Uniform Certified Public Accountants Exam (the CPA exam); and (c) the requisite amount of accounting work experience as mandated by each state, often two years or so.

Why Should I Become a CPA?

We'll talk about the requirements for becoming a CPA in more detail later, but first, you might be asking yourself, "Why should I go through all of this? Can't I be an accountant without being certified?"

What you can do without becoming a CPA

You most certainly can perform accounting functions without being certified, and there are many successful people in the profession who have taken this route. Non-certified accountants are not required to fulfill the five-year requirement; they aren't even required to have a degree in accounting (although, obviously, it helps). A traditional four-year degree is all that is necessary to be a non-certified accountant. The actual functions of an accountant are not, as the saying goes, rocket science, and complicated mathematics is rarely needed; thus, advanced certification might not seem necessary. Internal auditors, management accountants and tax personnel may all practice their professions without the CPA or any other professional designation,

Furthermore, many accounting professionals (CPAs and otherwise) contend that the CPA exam is nothing more than a rite of passage, an intense exercise in memorization that adds little actual value to your technical development as an accountant. These people generally feel that all of the information you crammed into your brain disappears once the exam is over. Many of them even said that this "brain drain" should happen since much of this information will never be seen in your actual practice; if you ever do need it, you can quickly look it up.

What you can't do

However, not being certified has a few significant drawbacks. Foremost among these is that it can be career limiting – most public accounting firms will not promote an auditor above a certain level (senior associate; these levels are discussed later in this guide) without at least passing the exam.

There are a couple of important reasons for this. First, only a CPA may sign an audit opinion. This signature is crucial, as it signifies that the auditor believes that the financial statements reasonably represent the company's actual financial position, giving the users of these statements more confidence that they can rely on them to make their decisions. Thus, an auditor without a CPA can not perform one of the most important activities of the profession.

Furthermore, a failure to pursue certification is often interpreted by public accounting firms as a lack of commitment to the profession, and few firms are willing to invest resources in someone who might leave the profession altogether (especially when there are so many others out there who are willing to pursue certification).

Another downside of not having a CPA is that you would miss out on the credibility that the certification carries. As with other advanced professional certifications, the CPA tends to give the stamp of "expert" in the eyes of the public and thus more perceived confidence in the accountant's abilities. Such credibility could mean the difference to a recruiter who's deciding between two otherwise comparable job candidates.

One final, ever-so-important downside of not having a CPA: you'll make less money. According to the staffing agency Robert Half International, the CPA can, on average, increase a candidate's base salary by 10 percent, with specialized fields (such as forensic accounting) commanding even higher salaries.

Now, this is not meant to scare you into pursuing the CPA, nor is it meant to suggest that you are a slacker if you don't pursue the CPA. You can still have a successful career in accounting without it. For example, public tax accountants generally do not sign off on audit opinions, and tax returns generally do not require the signature of a CPA. However, pursuing the CPA opens you up to many more opportunities and can only help a career in accounting. Thus, plans for certification should be seriously considered by anyone looking to break into the accounting field.

The 150-Hour Education Requirement

In 1998, the AICPA membership voted to increase the educational credentials required for certification. It implemented this requirement in response to increases in accounting, auditing and tax regulations, the increasing complexity of the business environment, the advance of technology and to improve the overall quality and breadth of work performed by CPAs. Now, in order to sit for the CPA exam in most states, you must have completed 150 credit hours, or five years, of college-level education. The additional year allows for increased development of communication, analytical and interpersonal proficiencies as well as technical competence.

According to some university career services offices, this requirement of a fifth year of education to sit for or practice as a CPA has inhibited the number of students entering the field. However, while the additional education might seem onerous to some, the good news is that starting salaries for accountants are spiking up to accommodate the increased education and skill levels.

How do you fulfill the requirement?

While the education requirement generally does not call for the attainment of a full master's degree, the most straightforward way of satisfying the requirement (and the way most schools have designed their accounting programs) involves a graduate degree. The 150-hour education requirement may usually be met in the following ways:

1. Combine an undergraduate accounting degree with a master's degree at the same school or a different one.

2. Combine an undergraduate degree in a non-accounting discipline with a master's degree in accounting or an MBA with a concentration in accounting.

3. Enroll in an integrated, five-year professional accounting school or program leading to a master's degree in accounting.

For a list of class topics most relevant to the profession, see the "Hiring Process and Interviews" chapter. Also see the AICPA's website at www.aicpa.org for more information.

Which jurisdictions support this requirement?

This requirement is in effect in 45 out of the 50 U.S. states, Puerto Rico and the District of Columbia. Currently, California, Colorado, Delaware, New Hampshire, Vermont and the Virgin Islands do not have the 150-hour requirement in place. In these states, only four years of education (an undergraduate degree) are required to sit for the exam. It should be noted that, since the general AICPA membership voted for and approved this requirement, it is expected that all U.S. states will eventually conform to these requirements.

Top accounting schools

There are hundreds of schools with well-developed accounting programs in the U.S. Below is a list of schools recognized for their undergraduate and graduate accounting programs. While this should not be considered an exhaustive list, these schools are generally considered the best in the nation for those pursuing accounting careers:

TOP ACCOUNTING SCHOOLS	
University of Illinois – Urbana Champaign	University of Texas at Austin
University of Michigan – Ann Arbor	University of Pennsylvania
University of Southern California	Brigham Young University – Provo
Northern Illinois University	University of Alabama
Texas A&M University	University of Florida
University of Wisconsin – Madison	University of Virginia
Indiana University	University of Notre Dame
Ohio State University	Arizona State University
University of Georgia	College of William & Mary
Michigan State University	Georgia State University
Miami (Ohio) University	University of Iowa
University of Arizona	Wake Forest University

The Exam

The CPA exam is a four-part exam — the accountant's version of running the gauntlet. As the AICPA requires that all four parts of the exam be passed, this represents the crucial step in becoming a certified public accountant, the culmination of those 150 credit hours of education.

Administered over two days, the Uniform Certified Public Accountants Exam is a grueling test designed to assess a candidate's knowledge of the following four areas:

- Business Environment and Concepts (BEC) – CPAs' professional responsibilities and the legal implications of business transactions, particularly as they relate to accounting and auditing.

- Auditing and Attestation (AUDIT) – Generally accepted auditing standards and procedures, and other standards related to attest engagements.

- Regulation – Federal taxation, ethics, professional and legal responsibilities and business law.

- Financial Accounting and Reporting (FAR) – Generally accepted accounting principles for business enterprises, not-for-profit organizations and government entities.

The exam is written by the Board of Examiners of the American Institute of Certified Public Accountants (AICPA). In May 1996, the exam became non-disclosed, which means that only selected questions from the exam are released to the public by the examiners. And as of 2004, the exam will be given in an exclusively computerized format. This new version of the exam is also slightly shorter (14 hours total as opposed to 15 1/2

CPA FAQ

When should I take the exam? Our recommendation – and the recommendation of virtually everyone in the business – is to begin preparing for the exam as soon as you graduate from college. You generally have the summer after graduation free, and the longer you wait, the harder it will be to motivate yourself to study. When you graduate, all of your accounting friends will be studying, too. If you do it together, it will most likely be a lot less painful. So, if you graduate in June, you might want to begin taking a preparation class (see below) in July. If you're working in public accounting, the firm will likely expect you to take the exam the first time it's offered after you start.

Will I get hired without it? Firms will hire you without your CPA, but the public accounting firms will expect you to pass the CPA before you can get promoted to manager, which typically comes around five years.

What happens if I fail? The exam is designed to be a rigorous challenge. Most people will tell you that, while the content of the exam is not unreasonably complicated, the sheer volume of knowledge that is tested makes the exam quite an ordeal. The numbers back this up: historically, only approximately 10 percent pass all four parts on the first try. Approximately 50 percent of the people who are sitting for the exam have taken it before. In other words, at least half the people who take the exam will fail at least one part of the exam on their first try.

If you don't pass all four parts on the first try, don't worry; it's not the end of the world. Take a look at your score and figure out what areas are your weaknesses. Focus your additional studying for the next exam on those areas. But no matter what, never give up. Each time you take the exam, you'll be able to identify areas of weakness, and if you take the time to brush up on those areas, without losing your existing strengths, you'll be more likely to pass.

When is the exam given? The exam is offered up to six days a week during January, February, April, May, July, August, October and November each year. Each two month testing period is called a window. Candidates make appointments for specific dates and times during a window at a regional testing center.

After the state board determines a candidate is eligible to sit for specific sections of the CPA Examination, the candidate will receive a Notice to Schedule (NTS).

The candidate can then register directly with a Prometric testing center to take one or more sections. Candidates can schedule test appointments online at www.prometric.com\cpa, or by calling 1-800-580-9648 (Candidate Services Call Center) or contacting their local test center.

What is the format? The exam is a combination of multiple-choice questions with four options, and condensed case studies called simulations. The format of each of the sections is as follows:

Section	Multiple-choice	Simulations
BEC	100%	0%
Audit	50-60%	30-40%
Regulation	50-60%	30-40%
FARE	50-60%	30-40%

The content of the exam is governed by the Content Specification Outlines. A summary of each section is as follows:

Business Environment and Concepts:

- Business structure (17-23%)
- Economic concepts (8-12%)
- Financial management (17-23%)
- Information technology (22-28%)
- Planning and measurement (22-28%)

Auditing and Attestation:

- Planning the engagement (22-28%)
- Internal controls (12-18%)
- Obtain and document information (32-35%)
- Review engagement and evaluate information (8-12%)
- Prepare communications (12-18%)

Regulation:

- Federal taxation entities (22-28%)
- Federal taxation of property transactions (8-12%)
- Federal procedures and accounting issue (8-12%)
- Ethics and professional responsibilities (15-20%)
- Business law (20-25%)

Financial Accounting & Reporting – Business Enterprises:

- Concepts and standards for financial statements (17-23%)

- Typical items in financial statements (27-33%)

- Specific types of transactions and events (27-33%)

- Acounting and reporting for governmental entities (8-12%)

- Accounting and reporting for non-governmental entities and not–for –profit organizations (8-12%)

How are the written sections evaluated? In place of essays, an assessment of written communication skills will be incorporated into the simulation portion of the revised examination. According to the CPA exam's website, the testing of written communication skills was identified by the most recent accounting practice analysis and supported by a special task force consisting of CPAs, psychometricians, and writing experts. In this portion of the exam, candidates must read a situation description and then write an appropriate document ("constructed response") relating to the situation. The instructions will state what form the document should take (such as a memo or letter) and its focus. The candidate's response should provide the correct information in writing that is clear, complete and professional. Constructed responses will be scored holistically, based on three general writing criteria: organization, development, and expression.

Is there an ethics component to the test? Some states require an ethics exam prior to certification, but this is an area of the test that is continuing to evolve. The regulation section of the CPA exam (formerly known as "Accounting and Reporting") now includes material on ethics and professional responsibility. And some states are adding a separate section on ethics to the CPA exam. Check the board of accountancy of the state in which you'll practice for ethics exam requirements.

Should I bring a calculator? You will be able to use the online calculator to perform standard financial calculations. Be sure you understand how to move the calculator on the screen.

How is the exam graded? The exam is graded on a scale from 0 to 99, and the passing standard remains 75. Conditional status may be granted to candidates who receive a passing grade on some but not all sections. Grades are released to the state boards after each two-month window of testing, and it is up to the state boards when to release those grades to the people who took the exam. You can sit for each section of the computerized exam individually, and in any order. You must pass all four sections within a rolling, 18-month period, which begins the day the first section is passed.

How do I sign up? CPA Examination Services administers the CPA exam for the following states:

Colorado, Connecticut, Delaware, Florida, Georgia, Hawaii, Indiana, Iowa, Kansas, Louisiana, Maine, Massachusetts, Michigan, Minnesota, Missouri, Montana, Nebraska, New Hampshire, New Jersey, New Mexico, New York, Ohio, Pennsylvania, Puerto Rico, Rhode Island, South Carolina, Tennessee, Utah, Vermont, Virginia, Wisconsin

They can be reached at 800-CPA-EXAM (800-272-3926). Washington State candidates should contact Castle Worldwide at 1-800-655-4845. Candidates from other states should contact their state board of accountancy, contact information for which is available at www.nasba.org.

Examinations must be scheduled at least six days in advance. CPA Examination sections are offered on a continual basis two out of every three months throughout the year (January, February, April, May, July, August, October, November) up to six days a week.

Preparing for the Exam

Most CPAs recommend taking some sort of review course in preparing for the CPA exam. While many people have successfully passed the exam by studying on their own, such a feat requires a high level of self-discipline. The revised exam's new format does make it easier to prepare for and take the exam, since most states now allow candidates to take one part of the exam at a time, but the exam's modified form and content reflects an expanded range of business topics and requires a more analytical approach to problem solving. So candidates must take extra care to ensure they understand the material and are adequately prepared for the test.

CPA review courses are a great way to impose this discipline, and they often provide their own little tricks to help you study certain parts of the exam. There are many different organizations that provide CPA review services. Some public accounting firms will subsidize your preparation costs or otherwise facilitate your preparations in some manner. Some of the more well-known CPA review courses are as follows:

Becker Conviser CPA Review. This is the most recognized review course among current CPAs. It was one of the first CPA review courses established, with over 40 years of experience. According to Becker, students who complete their course pass the exam at double the rate of non-Becker students and approximately one-third of all new CPAs are Becker CPA Review alumni. Becker offers four options to prepare for the exam: 1) interactive live instruction in Becker's multimedia classrooms (classes begin 4 months before the exam), 2) online instruction, 3) a self-paced CD ROM course, or 4) a 5-week intensive course. For schedules and registration, go to www.beckerconvisor.com or call 800-868-3900.

Kaplan CPA Review. Provides an online CPA course, providing students with flexibility, unlimited access and allows you to study at your own pace. For details, go to www.kaptest.com or call 800- CPA-2DAY.

MicroMash CPA Review. Provides you with a CPA course tailored to your weaknesses using "The MicroMash Way." The course provides online tools and printed review textbooks for additional study. MicroMash simulates the exam, with full-text answers and remedial help for all questions. The Homework Help Hotline provides staff CPAs and professors to answer questions promptly. MicroMash guarantees you will pass the exam next time you sit. This is the course of choice of most of the large accounting firms. For information, go to www.passmatrix.com or call (800) 272-7277.

Other companies that provide CPA review courses are:

Course	Phone	Web Information
Accounting Institute Seminars	(800) 635-9442	www.AIS-CPA.com
Gleim CPA Review	(800) 87-GLEIM	www.gleim.com
Lambers CPA Review	(800) 272-0707, (978) 685-5002	www.lamberscpa.com
Rigos CPA Review	(800) 636-0716; (206) 624-0716	www.rigosrev.com
Bisk CPA Review	(800) 404-7231	www.cpaexam.com
Wiley CPA Review	(800) 272-2100 (orders only)	www.wiley.com/cpa.html
Wise Guides, Inc.	(800) 713-2098, (216) 673-1616	www.wiseguides.com

There are a few key factors in taking the exam:

1) Make sure that you get the testing site that you want for the exam. To do this, register early, especially if you live in a highly populated area, so you can take the exam as soon as possible after completing your chosen method of review.

2) The week of the exam, get lots of rest, take a day off from studying, eat well. Pretend the morning of the exam is like any other morning and don't get too stressed out.

Another interesting recommendation we heard quite often: "Go for the Pass." In other words, while your competitive nature might lead you to try to get a high grade, your focus should be on simply passing. As one Big Four auditor explains, "There is no difference between a 75 and a 95 – the 75 certifies you just as well as the 95 does. It is one of the only exams you'll ever take where a 75 is just as satisfying as a 95, if not more so since you know you didn't over-study and go overboard." The gist of this suggestion is that the exam is difficult enough without killing yourself trying to cram every last bit of information into your head. On the CPA exam, grades don't matter – passing is the only thing that matters, and you should plan your preparation accordingly.

Visit the Vault Finance Career Channel at **www.vault.com/finance** – with
insider firm profiles, message boards, the Vault Finance Job Board and more.
VAULT CAREER LIBRARY **61**

Required Work Experience

Most states or jurisdictions require two years of public accounting audit experience for certification. The two years is a general guideline and is based on the number of hours worked on audits you've performed.

For auditors, the work experience requirement is fulfilled rather quickly as they spend virtually all of their work time on audits. For public accounting tax professionals, certification can take five years or longer since not all of their activities represent qualifying audit hours (for example, preparing a tax return is generally not considered audit work and does not count toward the CPA requirement).

Many states will also accept non-public accounting experience, but the number of years required is typically much higher, in some states as long as 15 years. It should be noted that some states, such as Maryland, do not have any work experience requirement and only require the fulfillment of education guidelines and the passing of the CPA exam. You should check with the board of accountancy of the state in which you'll be practicing to find out that state's exact work experience requirements.

ON THE JOB

Decrease your T/NJ Ratio
(Time to New Job)

Use the Internet's most targeted job search tools for finance professionals.

Vault Finance Job Board

The most comprehensive and convenient job board for finance professionals. Target your search by area of finance, function, and experience level, and find the job openings that you want. No surfing required.

VaultMatch Resume Database

Vault takes match-making to the next level: post your resume and customize your search by area of finance, experience and more. We'll match job listings with your interests and criteria and e-mail them directly to your inbox.

VAULT
> the most trusted name in career information™

On the Job

CHAPTER 6

According to the Bureau of Labor Statistics, there were nearly 1 million accountants and auditors in the United States in 2000. Of these, one out of four accountants work for accounting, auditing or bookkeeping firms. As such, most public accountants work in urban areas where public accounting firms and central or regional offices of their clients are concentrated. Many accountants and auditors are also unlicensed management accountants, internal auditors, government accountants and auditors and college and university faculty.

As an accountant, you will be asked to have high ethical standards, and to abide by those ethical standards with each and every decision that you make. As you progress from staff accountant to senior accountant to manager to partner, you will be asked to make tough ethical decisions that, as evidenced by Arthur Andersen and Enron, can affect the lives of each and every employee at the firm, as well as others, such as investors, who rely on your work.

Public Accounting Career Path

Public accounting generally entails a fairly rigid, hierarchical career path, as follows:

Audit

Staff Auditor (year 1-3). Staff auditors perform the meat of an audit, engaging in the often mentioned "ticking and tying" activities, i.e., analyzing and verifying the information contained in the myriad ledgers and statements provided by the client. Under the supervision of an audit senior, they will work with the client to obtain information and determine the validity and accuracy of the accounting records. It is the staff accountant's responsibility to investigate specific accounts assigned to them and to identify, resolve and document any material issues. Staff auditors will often start to direct small audits (and will be referred to as the "acting senior" on the engagement) in their second years.

Senior Auditor (year 3-6). Audit seniors are the glue that holds the audit together. They supervise the audit fieldwork of staff auditors and review their work products to ensure the audit is thorough and properly documented. They are responsible for resolving any accounting issues as they arise.

Visit the Vault Finance Career Channel at **www.vault.com/finance** — with insider firm profiles, message boards, the Vault Finance Job Board and more.

VAULT CAREER LIBRARY 65

Seniors are also responsible for identifying and documenting audit risks, creating and managing client relationships, administering budget issues and ensuring that the audit manager and partner are adequately informed of all relevant items. Specific senior auditor activities could include client meetings, partner and manager meetings, research on the relevant accounting standards and conversations with company headquarters.

Audit Manager (year 6+). The manager is ultimately responsible for managing client relationships. Although both the senior and staff auditors will be at the audit site each day during the audit, the manager will typically visit the audit site once a week, maybe more depending upon the status and time remaining to completion for the audit. The manager will perform a high level review of all the audit work after the senior is satisfied with the thoroughness and resolution of all issues. The manager supervises, trains and evaluates seniors and staff. They are also responsible for audit program approval, personnel scheduling, audit working paper review, financial statement disclosure/footnote approval, day-to-day client relationships and final determination of billings for engagements.

Partner/Senior Partner. Partners are responsible for overall client relationship and business development activities. Partners will sign the audit opinion and are responsible for the overall audit and coordination for the concurring partner review and any correspondence with headquarters. Partners will review and concur on all major accounting issues. They may visit the client site once on small audit engagements, if at all. The partner may be the only audit team member that attends audit committee meetings. Only 2 percent of the accountants entering CPA firms will reach the partner level. Partners typically purchase equity in the firm and share in all profits. Ordinarily, a professional must be a CPA to become a partner.

Tax

Tax Staff (year 1-3). Like their audit counterparts, tax staff personnel perform the meat of the tax work. They prepare tax returns, research tax issues and counsel clients on tax matters under the supervision of a tax senior and/or tax manager. Generally, tax staff do not have as much direct client contact as their audit counterparts. This level encompasses a significant amount of learning and training as the tax staff gets up to speed regarding basic aspects of income tax reporting, compliance and analysis.

Tax Senior (year 3-6). Tax seniors prepare and review tax returns, research tax issues, offer suggestions for tax planning, manage tax staff and study the

Internal Revenue Code and other applicable tax laws for potential client tax savings. They may also work with audit personnel in the preparation of tax items included in financial statement disclosure. This level also encompasses a significant amount of learning and training as the tax senior is expected to apply an increased technical tax comfort level to his or her client engagements in preparation for the manager level.

Tax Manager (year 6+). Unlike audit, where staff and seniors have the most extensive exposure to the client, client contact in tax engagements is generally the domain of the tax manager. Tax managers direct and review tax seniors and tax staff personnel; approve corporate tax returns prepared by tax staff; perform tax planning and research unusual tax matters; handle day-to-day client relationship issues; plan engagement billings and other administrative duties. They may also review tax items included in financial statement disclosure. Tax managers are expected to have a strong grasp of the technical tax issues applicable to their specific industry or tax function (e.g., State & Local, International). Many tax managers (and partners) are referred to as "Codeheads" for their ability to recite on command the exact Internal Revenue Code section applicable to a given tax issue. They are also expected to begin developing their marketing skills in preparation for the business development responsibilities of the Partner level.

Tax Partner/Senior Partner. Similar to their audit counterparts, tax partners are responsible for overall client relationship and business development activities. Tax partners often become specialists/experts for their deep knowledge of and experience with a specific industry or tax function.

Transferring

While many firms recruit hires by highlighting a young accountant's ability to gather experience in different service lines of the firm by transferring between audit and tax or business consulting, such behavior is often not encouraged and moves are usually not a frequent occurrence. Usually, such a transfer results in a move backward for a transferee in terms of having to learn a totally different set of work skills within their new group. Potential hires should not have the impression that transferring is expected or desirable.

Up or out

Because public accounting is a mature industry, persons entering with the idea of making a lifelong career of the profession should take note: the partnership tracks at the larger firms continue to lengthen and involve many

Visit the Vault Finance Career Channel at **www.vault.com/finance** — with
insider firm profiles, message boards, the Vault Finance Job Board and more.

VAULT CAREER LIBRARY   67

more steps along the path than ever before. Many professionals have found that transferring to a specialty line within a large accounting firm has offered them increased opportunities for advancement when compared to the traditional audit and tax departments. Be sure that you understand the current requirements to make partner within any specific firm you join. Also, know that it will likely be much harder than you are told to actually reach such a position due to these industry factors.

Traditionally, public accounting firms have held an "up or out" attitude in their retention practices. While this has recently changed slightly at the manager and partner levels, it still very much exists at the lower levels of these organizations. A public accounting firm employee needs to take an active role in monitoring and managing their career so that no news comes as a surprise. If the worst-case scenario comes true and an employee is let go (and it does happen more frequently than most firms speak of), then usually they are given a grace period to search for a new job. In general, public accounting firms view ex-employees as potential clients and treat them professionally.

Will an MBA help a career in accounting?

Generally, an MBA does not advance a career in accounting; rather, it positions an accountant to leverage his or her accounting proficiency to pursue other careers. Public accounting, to some degree, even eyes the advanced degree with some suspicion. According to one Big Four manager, "Whenever a staff person mentions an MBA to me, a yellow caution flag goes up in my mind. This is nothing against the degree itself, which clearly adds significant value to the person pursuing it, the kind of broad-based knowledge that should in theory enhance an accountant's perspective and performance on the job. But in reality, the time spent on an MBA is time spent away from developing the specific accounting knowledge needed in our profession. The MBA is a deep commitment of time and resources – dedicating so much to non-accounting topics is a signal to me that the person is thinking of leaving. What the MBA does is prepare someone to pursue other careers – it should come as no surprise that every accountant I've known who has earned the MBA has left the profession."

Nevertheless, an MBA degree can enhance an accountant's career, particularly that of a nonpublic accountant. One recruiter reports that many financial analyst positions often prefer or even require an MBA degree, as a financial analyst will often be a part of a cross-functional team that demands a comfort level with areas such as marketing, operations and management.

And, despite the suspicions of the manager previously quoted, an MBA degree does not automatically mean the end of a public accounting career. One Big Four CPA says that her firm even supported her desire to get the degree. "I've always enjoyed working at my firm, but I came to a point where I wanted to get a broader perspective on my job, something an MBA could give me. When I broached the subject with my partner, he was enthusiastic (he had always given me wonderful performance reviews) and nominated me for a process in which the firm would finance a full-time MBA for me so long as I agreed to work for the firm off-semester and for a set duration after earning my degree. After getting the MBA, I moved away from auditing (and my partner) and into a risk management role. I think in the view of my old partner, the firm should do whatever it takes to keep its top talent."

Nonpublic Accounting Career Path

Management accountants often start as cost accountants, junior internal auditors or trainees for other accounting positions. As they advance in their organizations, they may rise to accounting manager, controller, chief cost accountant, budget director or manager of internal auditing. Some also become treasurers, vice presidents of finance, chief financial officers or corporate presidents. Many senior corporate executives have a background in accounting, internal auditing or finance.

Financial accounting and reporting

Staff accountant (1-3 years). Financial accounting and reporting staff work under the direction of a senior accountant performing detailed work assignments in one or several of the following areas: receivables, payroll, payables, property, general ledger and financial statements

Senior accountant (3-6 years). Senior accountants supervise the work of staff accountants and are responsible for special reports and financial analyses.

Accounting manager (6+ years). Accounting managers assist the controller and are often responsible for one of the functional areas such as financial accounting or budgetary planning and control. They direct the work of personnel involved in detailed accounting entries, internal financial reporting and financial statements.

Internal audit

Staff internal auditors (1-3 years). Internal audit staff works under the direction of seniors and managers in conducting compliance audits and tests internal controls and information systems.

Senior internal auditors (3-6 years). Internal audit seniors supervise the testing of internal control and accounting information systems. They often conduct statistical samples of document approval, perform tests to uncover and perform operational audits for profit improvement recommendations.

Internal audit managers (6+ years). Internal audit managers direct the staff responsible for systematically sampling the adequacy and reliability of internal control systems. They make recommendations for changes as needed, and ensure that company policies and procedures are followed and establish the proper techniques to discover and prevent fraud.

Executive level

Controller. The controller functions as the Chief Accounting Executive responsible for organizing, directing and controlling the work of the accounting personnel in collecting, summarizing and interpreting financial data for the use of management, creditors, investors and taxing authorities. As a member of top management, the controller helps develop forecasts for projects, measure the actual performance against operating standards and interprets the results of operations for all levels of management.

Chief Financial Officer. The CFO advises the president of the organization with respect to financial reporting, financial stability and liquidity, and financial growth. The CFO directs and supervises the work of the controller, treasurer, and sometimes the internal auditing manager. Other duties include maintenance of relationships with stockholders, financial institutions and the investment community. The CFO contributes to the overall organization planning, policy development and implementation.

The training difference

One crucial difference between private and public accounting firms lies in the amount and depth of training. Many of the Big Four and the larger regional firms have dedicated training centers with full-time educational staffs, seminars led by subject-specific experts, or both. A new public accountant can expect to receive approximately three to four weeks of formal educational training in his or her first year.

This training doesn't even include the "on-the-job" type learning prevalent within the industry. The majority of the skills necessary for success at public accounting are taught through the mentoring process with seniors, managers and partners doing the tutoring. So to get the most from your mentors, ask plenty of questions.

The Typical Day in Accounting

The day of a staff accountant will vary significantly based on the time of year, type of work being performed and the status of the work being performed. The length of the day can vary from eight hours a day when on an engagement with time to spare to a 20-hour day on engagements with tight time constraints.

In order to really understand the life of an auditor, you have to understand the audit cycle and the times that are the busiest for accountants. The length of the day and week and the stress level of those days will vary greatly depending on the client, the time of year and the audit team.

During busy season, most audit firms have a rule that no one is allowed to schedule any vacation, regardless of the reason. So don't schedule your wedding during busy season, and don't plan to go skiing a lot if you're working on public clients with a December 31 fiscal year. Plan on saying goodbye to your friends and family, home-cooked meals and relaxing afternoons on the porch.

Plan to catch up on your social life as the busy season ends. After busy season, work will slow down significantly; you may even have some time when you're not assigned to a client. Enjoy that downtime while you can.

Visit the Vault Finance Career Channel at **www.vault.com/finance** — with
insider firm profiles, message boards, the Vault Finance Job Board and more.

V\ULT CAREER LIBRARY   **71**

A Typical Long-Term Engagement Schedule		
September – October	Senior manager	Plan the audit: • Identify audit risks • Determine hours, budgets, etc. • Draft audit timelines
January – April	Entire audit team	Complete the audit Issue financial statements and press releases
	Partner only	Attend the audit committee meeting

If you're working on short-term engagements, you will inevitably work on more than one engagement at a time during busy season. Small clients will drag on well into other audits and will continue to haunt you as busy season progresses. If you work on a long-term engagement, you may be working on only one client, but within that client, don't be surprised if there are 30 to 50 different sets of financial statements that need to be reviewed. It is the nature of managers and partners to work on multiple engagements, but they're not involved in the nitty-gritty of the audit. They tend to remain at a higher level reviewing and discussing issues rather than all of the audit work.

Day in the Life – Auditor Intern

Following is a description of a typical day as experienced by an intern at an auditing department at one of the Big Four firms:

9:00 a.m.: If I'm unassigned, go to the office to check e-mails and phone messages. If assigned, arrive at the client site (but days usually start around 8 a.m.). At the client's office, I'll be meeting the client on a new job (usually the controller, other accounting personnel or pension plan administrator), getting to know where the files are, networking my laptop with my co-workers', and getting to know the job. I'll also find out the first account I'll be working on – usually equipment, accounts receivable or attributes testing for pension plans. My senior will usually sit down with me for about a half-hour, and walk through most everything I'd be doing on the account (using the audit program and last year's work papers).

10:00 a.m.: Still working through my first account or attribute test. I stop lots to ask questions, which is encouraged. Sometimes the answer to my question has to be found with the client, and sometimes I'm sent by myself to approach the client. This helps in building a relationship with the client (if I end up working here full-time, I'll definitely see them the next year), confidence skills, and analytical skills in learning to ask the right question.

11:00 a.m.: Probably still working through the same account. Some larger accounts, like accounts receivable, take days and days. Around 11:30, one of my engagement team members will mention lunch and that will be discussed for a while.

12:00 p.m.: Lunch! A lot of variety here. I've eaten at everything from fancy places to fast food. Usually, if clients or partners are involved, lunch is taken care of. This is the time to get to know your team on a more personal level, which is always enjoyable.

1:00 p.m.: Back to work. Get some caffeine to fight off the after-lunch slump. There's a possibility that I might be starting something new at this point, and thus the cycle of explanation begins again.

2:00 p.m.: Still working though the accounts. If unassigned and in the office, there's a good possibility I'll be picked up on a small in-office job. These jobs usually consist of photocopying, typing and pulling files. It isn't bad to work these types of jobs; I enjoy the exposure I get to people I would not work with otherwise, like those in our tax department. If unassigned and not on a job, I'll be working through an online tutorial, surfing the Web, writing e-mails or chatting with friends. Unassigned time can get pretty boring, but I luckily don't have too much of it.

3:00 p.m.: Audit, audit, audit. I try to take lots of notes on my work towards the end of the day so I'll be set when I come in the next morning.

4:00 p.m.: Making sure all my work papers are organized, understandable, and that the notes make sense. If at the end of an engagement, I will always sit down with my senior and explain exactly what I had finished, where I left off, and what still needs to be done. I try to always write out all of that too, just so the message got across.

5:00 p.m.: I'll usually leave pretty close to 5 p.m., definitely by 5:30. On a few jobs I had, I left as early at 3:00.

6:00 p.m.: Fighting the traffic home or to an intern event.

One size does not fit all

The size of the audit team varies based on the size of the engagement. A small audit team will consist of a staff auditor, a senior auditor, a manager and a partner. On a small audit, the manager and partner may visit the client site once during the audit period. Small audits can range from three days to two weeks at the client site. A large client can have a year-round audit team consisting of more than one team member at each level. Teams usually have a pyramid structure, with more staff accountants than seniors and managers.

Day in the Life – Tax Staff

Following is a description of a typical day as experienced by a tax staff professional at a Big Four firm.

8:00 a.m.: I like to get in a little earlier than others (most other people in the office get in around 9:00). This gives me a chance to check e-mail and voice mail, take care of administrative tasks, check my open items from the previous day and make a general plan for my day. If things are slow, this is the time I read *The Wall Street Journal* or other periodicals for news regarding my clients.

9:00 a.m.: The office is jumping and the phone calls are starting to come in. At this time, I often have meetings with my manager and senior to discuss work in progress. These meetings will usually touch on the following: list of open (i.e., unfinished) items on tax returns, general tax matters for clients, tax technical issues requiring further research, and client management issues and administration. My manager will generally prioritize these items and the senior and I will form a plan of attack.

10:00 a.m.: As the tax staff, I'll most likely address the tax return open items and perform any research on technical tax issues; the senior will deal more often with general tax matters and client relationship items. Preparing a corporate tax return is relatively straightforward. While corporate tax returns can be quite complex, you can more or less prepare a corporate return line-by-line, same as an individual return.

The primary challenge in preparing a corporate return is ensuring that you have complete, full and accurate information from the client. This is more daunting than it sounds. Information necessary to complete a tax return can come from numerous sources within a company, not just the accounting and tax departments. The larger the company, the more potentially difficult it is to get all of your information. As a result, most of the hours I bill on tax return preparation projects are spent not on actually preparing the return, but on tracking down all of the necessary information. I'll generally put together an information request that, after a brief review by the manager, I will e-mail or fax to the client.

Tax research is generally more straightforward than tax return preparation. The firm has every possible tax research tool and source, from print to electronic to online to human. The ironic thing is that most of the research items you get at this level are ones for which answers are already known. Managers give you these research items pretty much knowing what the likely outcomes will be: you just confirm the suspicion with actual Internal Revenue

Code sources, tax court cases or other citations. Sometimes you'll get a unique and challenging assignment, but the new topics are usually researched by groups within the firm that specialize in that technical area.

In any case, these activities could easily take up the rest of my day, depending on how cooperative the client is or how difficult the information is to get.

1:00 p.m.: Lunch.

2:00 p.m.: Another e-mail and voice mail check, after which I'll resume my activities from the morning. At this point, I probably will have spent a good amount of time on the phone with client personnel trying to track down information. In the best-case scenario, the client will have sent me back my information request with at least some information; realistically, the information request will get back to me no earlier than two or three days after I send it.

I'll most likely spend some time making sure that the information we do have is correctly entered into the tax preparation software our firm uses. And at this point, I'll hopefully have some answers or information regarding the research I performed on the tax issues. If so, I'll try to schedule some time with my senior and/or manager later this afternoon to discuss my findings. Throughout the day, I'll be gathering and organizing my work papers for inclusion in the client's file.

4:00 p.m.: If all goes well, I'm having a brief meeting with my senior and/or manager discussing the research I performed. This discussion will hammer out how this issue could affect the tax return. Often, this discussion will result in my drafting of a technical memorandum that outlines the issue and our findings. These memos are pretty interesting because they represent more strategic and interpretive thought than plugging numbers into a tax return. The research and memos feel like the real meat of tax work.

6:00 p.m.: Finishing touches on my draft memo (the manager always has modifications), organizing my work papers, checking off my open items for tomorrow, and preparing my timesheet for the day. This will all probably take me 30-40 minutes, and then I'm off home. Incidentally, I should note that I'm usually working on multiple tax returns and other projects at one time. So there's usually a lot of juggling going on, putting a premium on my time management and organizational skills. And if this was busy season, my leaving time wouldn't be anywhere near 6:00 p.m. – it'd probably be closer to 11:00 p.m.

The typical public accounting project cycle

Young accounting staffers with dreams of making boardroom presentations to clients should postpone those dreams for a while. Typically, work for young staffers remains administrative. Partners and senior managers handle the delivery of the "pitch" to clients and prospective clients.

Once a firm lands a client, the partners of the firm will form an engagement team for that particular job. Industry experience and schedule availability are the main criteria for selection for a particular engagement. Depending on the length and complexity of an assignment, multiple managers and a senior may be selected to complete the work.

During the initial stage of the work, a project is usually referred to as a "first time through," and firms will expend extra effort to understand a client's business and offer them improvement points on their current work processes. This step is especially interesting for the younger professionals, since it gives them much more of a chance to dissect a company's operations and gain a better understanding of how the work products of different departments flow together. This is the stage when accountants and consultants produce books outlining the client's procedures. This documentation is used in subsequent years and only updated for any changes that may have taken place in the company's operations. These briefing documents reduce the workload on subsequent jobs for recurring clients.

The analytical techniques used during an audit don't differ in their application, but the extent of their application will depend on how knowledgeable an auditor is about a particular client's operations. During a first-time audit, an accountant will employ many more statistical tests.

The culmination of the audit process usually results in the issuance of an audit opinion on a client's financial statements. The auditors will also make a presentation to the audit committee of the company's board of directors. During this meeting, the opinion will be presented, along with any management recommendations the public accounting firm has. Usually, only the manager and partners attend such meetings, although it is not unusual for very experienced seniors to attend on occasion. In reality, the partners usually use the meeting as a chance to highlight other potential services that they could be selling a company. Additionally, they enjoy the chance to market to board members who may work for other corporations.

Our Survey Says: Accounting Lifestyle

Hours

The lifestyle for accountants can vary significantly throughout the year by client and level within the firm. Overall, the hours required by the profession are relatively reasonable and predictable. At most times during the year, the lifestyle is relatively good, eight- to 10-hour days and 45- to 50-hour weeks with exceptions for some clients. During busy season, you can expect to work anywhere from eight to 20 hours a day. Busy season for public clients generally lasts from January to April; for government clients, July through August. For tax compliance engagements, busy season is the six- to eight-week period before the various major tax filing deadlines (March 15, April 15, September 15, October 15).

Travel

The high level of client contact required by an audit tends to result in a significant amount of travel for auditors, especially seniors and staff who are often dedicated to a client for an extended period of time. Travel estimates range anywhere from 30 percent to nearly full-time for some auditors. Managers also may travel quite a bit, although they may move more frequently among their different clients.

On the contrary, public tax staff and seniors tend to travel much less frequently. The information that tax professionals need to prepare tax returns can often be either sent to them by the client or provided by the client's auditors (often from the same accounting firm). However, tax planning and consulting engagements may often require significant, or even full-time, travel.

For private and governmental accountants, travel requirements are much more varied, dependent on a myriad of factors including the nature of their function or business. Some may never leave their offices in their careers, while others may spend a significant amount of time on the road. Government accountants may travel frequently to perform audits and other analyses at government facilities nationwide.

Dress code

Dress codes in public accounting are quite reasonable. The Big Four firms have gone to a full-time casual dress code while in the office, with formal business attire appropriate for in-office client meetings (many in the Big Four keep suits in their offices). When going out to a client site, public accounting firms generally require their auditors to dress in a similar manner to their client. The dress code of accountants in private companies varies depending upon the industry, ranging from jeans and polo shirts in the entertainment industry to full business attire at financial services firms.

Compensation

According to the U.S. Bureau of Labor Statistics, in 2002, the median annual salary of accountants and auditors was $47,000, with the median entry-level salary in public accounting around $29,000. The middle half of the occupation earned between $37,210 and $61,630; the top 10 percent earned over $82,230. According to a survey by the National Association of Colleges and Employers (NACE), people with undergraduate accounting degrees received starting offers averaging $40,000 in 2003; holders of masters in accounting degrees averaged $43,000. While private sector salaries usually approximate those in public accounting, they are slightly lower in government. Salaries tend to be higher in major cities. The following table shows public accounting averages, compiled in 2003 by staffing frim Robert Half International.

Level	Public Accounting Average
Entry Level	$29-40,000
Junior Staff	$34-49,000
Senior Staff	$41-61,500
Manager	$47-78,750
Senior Manager	$66-197,500

In the federal government, the starting annual salary for junior accountants and auditors was $23,442 in 2003. Candidates with superior academic records might start at $29,037, while applicants with master's degrees or two

Visit the Vault Finance Career Channel at **www.vault.com/finance** — with insider firm profiles, message boards, the Vault Finance Job Board and more.

VAULT CAREER LIBRARY   79

years of professional experience started at \$35,518. Overall, accountants employed by the federal government in all non-supervisory, supervisory and managerial positions averaged \$69,370 in 2003.

Perks

The accounting industry doesn't match investment banking or law in terms of employee perks, but firms still try to make life easier for their employees. Naturally, life is sweeter as you move up the ladder. Some such benefits are:

Staff

- A per diem for expenses while traveling. Intended to cover meals and entertainment, these per diems can be used however employees like – in other words, no receipts are required.

- Plenty of free meals (usually eaten in a conference room at a client site).

- Use of a personal computer – though in most cases the firm retains ownership of the unit, in the event that you quit or otherwise leave the firm.

- The opportunity to travel and retain your frequent flier miles. Opinions vary as to whether extensive travel is ultimately a perk or a chore.

Seniors

Seniors have all of the perks of a staffer along with a bonus that is based upon the results of their office. The bonus plans differ greatly from firm to firm, so it's wise to ask about the policy regarding contingent compensation.

Managers

At this level of responsibility, accountants are usually eligible for bonuses based upon personal performance, including hours billed and work sold to clients. The travel in this position tends to cover more destinations but for shorter periods of time, since the professional is usually supervising multiple engagements simultaneously.

Partners

Compensation and perks at this level can be fabulous, but vary based upon a person's ability to generate fee-based revenue. Also, equity ownership in the firm is often offered to partners, though some may still be salaried employees of the organization.

Vacations

One benefit of working at a public accounting firm is that the amount of vacation given to an undergraduate hire is much greater than at many other companies. Sadly, the opportunity to go on vacation decreases as you grow in responsibility within a firm. However, early on, the summer generally presents many opportunities to take vacations. As one former Deloitte & Touche auditor says, "I never would have received four weeks of time off with any other employer. Also, I was fortunate enough to have been given the opportunity to take much of that time consecutively so that I could travel for an extended period overseas during my second year with the firm."

Social events

The amount of intra-office socializing, such as parties and galas depends on the office. However, teams usually hold an end-of-engagement party following large engagements. Additionally, you will get the chance to entertain clients, such as corporate accounting staffs, during the year. You should note that these opportunities increase with experience and responsibility. Usually, staff and seniors are not involved in marketing the firm. Social opportunities with peers are usually quite varied, since most firms tend to have many personnel around the same age.

Support staff/services

Much of the office administrative work is handled by the young public accounting staff, while travel arrangements and other large expense items for a firm are usually handled by the office for oversight purposes. At client sites, the most junior member(s) of the team handle most of the administrative duties. This person is generally responsible for copies and other menial chores such as fetching food.

Visit the Vault Finance Career Channel at **www.vault.com/finance** — with
insider firm profiles, message boards, the Vault Finance Job Board and more.

V/\ULT CAREER LIBRARY   **81**

Succeeding in the Firm

So, you're pretty good at math, you've taken the required 150 credit hours of education, and have passed the CPA exam – you're well on your way to a lucrative career in accounting, right? Not exactly. These accomplishments, while commendable, are merely the baseline requirements for success in the accounting profession. There are other skills that an accountant must have or develop in order to truly add value to their clients and organizations.

Not just bean counters

It is a common perception that accountants, as the "bean counters," must be good with numbers. While a proficiency in mathematics is important, it is not the only skill that this profession requires. Accountants must be able to analyze, compare and interpret facts and figures quickly. They must be able to communicate and present their findings clearly to many different levels within an organization, both their own and those of their clients. They must also be good at working in teams and with clients as well as with computers and other information systems. Legal knowledge and foreign language skills are also becoming more important as businesses globalize and become more team-oriented. Finally, as glaringly illustrated by Enron and other scandals, accountants must maintain high ethical standards and perform their duties with the utmost integrity, as millions of financial statement users rely on their work products.

Just saying "No"

Beyond these obvious skills, there is one crucial skill that accountants, especially those in public accounting, must learn: the ability to say "no." As simple as this sounds, this skill will not only help the new accountant to remain sane, it will allow the accountant to manage the expectations of supervisors and client personnel alike. Inevitably, the new accountant will be pulled this way and that by the demands of different managers and partners, as well as those of his clients. With only 24 hours in a day, the accountant will have to learn to prioritize under pressure and say "no" to some of these demands without creating team or client discord. It is subtle, indeed, but necessary to avoid being stretched too thin and/or performing jobs inadequately.

Is There Life After Public Accounting?

CHAPTER 7

In addition to the career tracks already discussed, accounting can provide an excellent foundation for careers in investment banking and corporate finance. An accountant can pick up any set of financial statements and identify areas for improvement or potential problem areas for evaluation. These are important skills for investment bankers. An accountant knows what's important to an auditor or a tax accountant and can make the interactions with external auditors smoother each year. A manager or partner at a public accounting firm can become the CFO or CEO of a public firm. These managers have exposure to a variety of industries, a variety of products, and strategies at both successful and floundering companies. These experiences will provide accountants the ability to analyze strategic alternatives for growing the business and sustaining profitability.

Cash flows are essential to keeping any business alive — accountants understand the ins and outs of a cash flow. They understand what's important to cash flows and what will affect the company's ability to repay its debt and meet analyst expectations. All of these are important skills that make accountants valuable in any job, not just investment banking and corporate finance. The switch to various industries is discussed in detail below.

Investment Banking

Accountants make good investment bankers for several reasons. The strong analytical and quantitative skills developed in public accounting provide an excellent basis for completing investment banking-type work. The easiest and most popular way to make the switch from accounting to investment banking is to get an MBA and pursue an internship and full-time job in investment banking. An MBA will give you the relevant finance skills and open doors that otherwise would be difficult to open. Getting hired as an investment banking associate after an MBA is a normal career progression and is more likely to happen than a transition from the lower levels of public accounting.

Corporate Finance

A few years of public accounting experience will prepare you well for the transition to corporate finance. Public accounting will provide you the exposure to a variety of industries, allowing you to determine which industries and types of work interest you. A transition to the financial reporting role at a corporation is the easiest one for accountants. Other opportunities for corporate finance positions include the treasury department and internal audit (see segmentation of accounting careers).

Other Industries and Functions

Accounting will also prepare you to work in a variety of other jobs where the skills learned in college and through work experience will allow you to exceed expectations. The skills you learned will allow you to excel in consulting, marketing and brand management. While these careers are not completely focused on finance and accounting skills, you will nonetheless find yourself looking at financial information more often than you would expect. You will benefit from your ability to understand and evaluate the financial statements. The most straightforward means by which to transition into consulting or marketing from an accounting career is by getting an MBA.

Other specific functions for accountants include: internal control systems design, budget analysis, cost estimation, loan analysis and approval, financial analysis, personal financial advisory, tax examination and collection and management consulting.

ACCOUNTING EMPLOYERS

BDO Seidman, LLP

130 E. Randolph Street
Suite 2800
Chicago, IL 60601
Phone: (312) 240-1236
Fax: (312) 240-3329
www.bdo.com

MAJOR DEPARTMENTS & PRACTICES

Assurance
Consulting
Corporate Finance
Financial Advisory
Financial Recovery Services
Healthcare
Internal Audit/Risk Consulting
Litigation Services
Taxation (Domestic, International)
Real Estate
SEC

THE STATS

CEO: Jack Weisbaum
Chairman of the Board: Wayne Kolins
Employer Type: Private partnership
(independent member of BDO
International)
Revenue: $365 million (FYE 6/04)
No of. Employees: 1,947
No. of Offices: 36

KEY COMPETITORS

Deloitte & Touche
Ernst & Young
KPMG
McGladrey & Pullen
PricewaterhouseCoopers

EMPLOYMENT CONTACT

130 E. Randolph, Ste. 2800
Chicago, IL 60601
Phone: 312-240-1236
Fax: 312-240-3311
www.bdo.com/careers

Visit the Vault Finance Career Channel at **www.vault.com/finance** — with
insider firm profiles, message boards, the Vault Finance Job Board and more.

VAULT CAREER LIBRARY   87

Berdon LLP

360 Madison Avenue
New York, NY 10017
Phone: (212) 832-0400
Fax: (212) 371-1159
www.berdonllp.com

DEPARTMENTS

Advertising
Architecture/Engineering Firms
Bankruptcy and Insolvency
Berdon Healthcare Consulting
Corporate Finance
Disaster Preparedness
Entertainment
Estate Planning
Family/Owner-Managed Businesses
Growing Business
Internal Auditing & 404 Compliance
Law Firm
Litigation & Business Valuation
Nonprofit
Personal Wealth Management,
  Personal Business Management,
  Financial Consulting
Personal Wealth Management for
  Attorneys
Real Estate
Real Estate Institutional Investors

THE STATS

Managing Partner: Stanley Freundlich
Employer Type: Private partnership
Revenue: $64.0 million (FYE 12/03)
No. of Employees: 350+
No. of Offices: 2

EMPLOYMENT CONTACT

Melanie Villaruel
Human Resources Administrator
Berdon LLP
360 Madison Avenue
New York, NY 10017
E-mail: mvillaruel@berdonllp.com

BKD LLP

Hammons Tower
901 E. St. Louis Street, Suite 1800
P.O. Box 1900
Springfield, MO 65801-1900
Phone: (417) 831-7283
Fax: (417) 831-4763
www.bkd.com

DEPARTMENTS

Accounting
Assurance
Audit
Consulting
Financial Advisory
Tax

THE STATS

Managing Partner: William E. Fingland Jr.
Employer Type: Private partnership
Revenue: $230.6 million (FYE 5/04)
No. of Employees: 1,500
No. of Offices: 27

KEY COMPETITORS

American Express Tax and Business
Services
BDO Seidman
Crowe Chizek
Grant Thornton

EMPLOYMENT CONTACT

Randy Hultz
Career Development Director
(417) 831-7283
rhultz@bkd.com

Cherry, Bekaert & Holland L.L.P.

1700 Bayberry Court
Suite 300
Richmond, VA 23226-3791
Phone: (804) 673-4224
Fax: (804) 673-4290
www.cbh.com

DEPARTMENTS

Audit & Accounting
Business Valuations
Cost Segregation Studies
Employee Benefit Plan Compliance
Estates & Trusts
Financial Planning & Advisory
Fraud & Forensic Studies
Internal Auditing & Outsourcing
International Tax
Litigation Support
Mergers & Acquisitions
Sarbanes – Oxley Implementation
State & Local Tax (SALT)
    Consulting
Strategic Management Services
Tax Planning & Compliance
Telecommunications Consulting

THE STATS

Managing Partner: Howard Kies
Employer Type: Private partnership
Revenue: $58.0 million (FYE 4/04)
No. of Employees: 535
No. of Offices: 17

EMPLOYMENT CONTACT

Wendy Berenson
Recruiting Manager
E-mail: wberenson@cbh.com

Experienced professionals:
See the "Careers" section of
www.cbh.com

Clifton Gunderson LLP

301 SW Adams Street
Suite 600
Phone: (309) 671-4560
Fax: (206) 671-4576
www.cliftoncpa.com

DEPARTMENTS

Accounting
Assurance
Corporate Finance
Financial Services
International
Management Consulting
Succession Planning
Tax Services
Technology Consulting
Valuation & Forensic

THE STATS

CEO: Carl R. George
Employer Type: Private partnership
Revenue: $160.0 million (FYE 5/04)
No. of Employees: 1,502
No. of Offices: 42

KEY COMPETITORS

BDO Seidman
Grant Thornton
McGladrey & Pullen
Moss Adams

EMPLOYMENT CONTACT

www.cliftoncpa.com/careers

Visit the Vault Finance Career Channel at **www.vault.com/finance** — with
insider firm profiles, message boards, the Vault Finance Job Board and more.

VAULT CAREER LIBRARY   91

Crowe Chizek and Co. LLC

330 East Jefferson Boulevard
South Bend, IN 46624-0007
Phone: (574) 232-3992
Fax: (574) 236-8692
www.crowechizek.com

DEPARTMENTS

Assurance
Consulting
Risk Management
Specialty Services
Tax
Technology

THE STATS

CEO: Mark Hildebrand
Employer Type: Private partnership
Revenue: $286.2 million (FYE 5/04)
No. of Employees: 1,400
No. of Offices: 19

KEY COMPETITORS

BDO Seidman
Clifton Gunderson
McGladrey & Pullen

EMPLOYMENT CONTACT

Crowe Chizek and Company LLC
Firmwide Recruitment
320 E. Jefferson Blvd.
South Bend, IN 46624
Fax: (574) 236-7609
E-mail: recruiting@crowechizek.com or
campus_recruiting@crowechizek.com

Deloitte & Touche USA LLP

1633 Broadway
New York, NY 10019
Phone: (212) 492-4000
Fax: (212) 492-4154
www.deloitte.com

SERVICES

Asian Business Services
Assurance
Consulting
Corporate Governance &
    Accountability
Financial Advisory Services
Merger & Acquisition Services
Radio Frequency Identification
Risk Consulting
Sarbanes-Oxley
Tax Services

THE STATS

U.S. CEO: James Quigley
Employer Type: Private partnership
(U.S. member firm of Deloitte Touche
Tohmatsu)
Revenue: $6.87 billion (FYE 6/04)
No. of Employees: 30,000
No. of Offices: 107 (in 90 cities)

KEY COMPETITORS

Ernst & Young
KPMG
PricewaterhouseCoopers

EMPLOYMENT CONTACT

www.deloitte.com/careers

Visit the Vault Finance Career Channel at **www.vault.com/finance** — with
insider firm profiles, message boards, the Vault Finance Job Board and more.

VAULT CAREER LIBRARY

93

Dixon Hughes PLLC

1829 Eastchester Dr.
High Point, NC 27261-2612
Phone: (336) 889-5156
www.dixon-hughes.com

DEPARTMENTS

Assurance
Business Valuation and Litigation
Corporate Finance
Corporate Governance
Dealership Services Consulting
Dixon Hughes Wealth Advisors
EDP & Internet Assurance
Family Business
Fraud & Forensic
Human Capital Management
Information Technology
Management Advisory Services
   (MAS)
Organizational Development
PROFIT
Retirement Plan Solutions
Sarbanes – Oxley Compliance
Software Solutions
Tax Services

THE STATS

Executive Members: Ken Hughes &
Eddie Sams
Employer Type: Limited liability
partnership
Revenue: $96.1 million (FYE 5/04)
No. of Employees: 880
No. of Offices: 26

EMPLOYMENT CONTACT

Kim Bullard
Sanford, NC
Phone: (919) 776-0555

Courtney Thomas
Greenville, NC
Phone: (864) 213-5355
www.dixon-hughes.com/recruitment.htm

Eide Bailly LLP

406 Main Avenue, Suite 300
P.O. Box 2545
Fargo, ND 58108-2545
Phone: (701) 239-8500
Fax: (701) 239-8600
www.eidebailly.com

DEPARTMENTS

Accounting Services
Audit Services
Business Brokerage
Business Consulting
Business Valuation
Corporate Finance
Employee Benefit Plan Compliance
Farm Accounting & Tax
Medical Practice Management
Peer Review Services
SEC Services
Tax Services
Wealth Transfer Services

THE STATS

CEO: Jerry Topp
Employer Type: Limited Liability Partnership
Revenue: $62.7 million (FYE 4/04)
No. of Employees: 652
No. of Offices: 11

EMPLOYMENT CONTACT

Nicole Campbell
E-mail: ncampbell@eidebailly.com

Visit the Vault Finance Career Channel at **www.vault.com/finance** — with
insider firm profiles, message boards, the Vault Finance Job Board and more.

VAULT CAREER LIBRARY

95

Eisner LLP

750 Third Avenue
New York, NY 10017
Phone: (212) 949-8700
Fax: (212) 891-4100
www.eisnerllp.com

DEPARTMENTS

Audit and Accounting
Corporate Tax Planning
Individual and Family Tax Planning
Corporate Finance
Legal Support Services
Personal Financial Services
Small Business Services
Employee and Executive Benefits
Human Resource Strategies
Corporate Restructuring
Bankruptcy and Insolvency Services
E-Commerce
Information Technology Consulting
Software Selection and
    Implementation
Operations Management
Data and Telecommunications
Networks

THE STATS

CEO and Managing Partner: Richard Eisner
Employer Type: Private partnership
Revenue: $73.2 million (FYE 1/04)
No. of Employees: 400
No. of Offices: 3

EMPLOYMENT CONTACT

www.eisnerllp.com/careers/careers.cfm

Ernst & Young LLP

5 Times Square
New York, NY 10036
Phone: (212) 773-3000
www.ey.com

DEPARTMENTS

Assurance & Advisory Business
Services
Emerging & Growth Markets
Human Capital
Online Services
Specialized Services
Tax
Transaction Advisory Services

THE STATS

Chairman and CEO: James S. Turley
Employer Type: Private partnership
(U.S. member firm of Ernst & Young
International)
Revenue (Global): $14.5 billion (FYE
6/04)
No. of Employees (U.S.): 23,000
No. of Locations (U.S.): 95

KEY COMPETITORS

Deloitte & Touche
KPMG
PricewaterhouseCoopers

EMPLOYMENT CONTACT

Visit the firms careers site at:
www.ey.com/us/careers

Goodman & Company

One Commercial Place
Norfolk, VA 23510-2119
Phone: (757) 624-5100
Fax: (757) 624-5233
www.goodmanco.com

DEPARTMENTS

Accounting
Auditing and Accounting
Business Valuation
Employee Benefit Services
Estate Planning
Financial Planning
Management Consulting
Tax Credits and Financial
Incentives
Tax Planning and Preparation
Consulting
Business Planning
Government Contract Consulting
Human Resource Consulting
   Services
Organization & Operational Reviews
Profit Enhancement
Strategic Planning

THE STATS

Managing Partner: Pat Viola
Employer Type: Private company
Revenue: $44.5 million (FYE 6/04)
No. of Employees: 450
No. of Offices: 10

EMPLOYMENT CONTACT

www.goodmanco.com/goodco/careers.asp

Grant Thornton LLP

175 West Jackson Boulevard
20th Floor
Chicago, IL 60604
Phone: (312) 856-0001
Fax: (312) 565-4719
www.grantthornton.com

DEPARTMENTS

Assurance and Advisory Services
Compensation and Benefits
International
M&A Advisory Services
Management Advisory Services
Tax Consulting Services
Valuation Services

THE STATS

CEO: Edward E. Nusbaum
Employer Type: Private partnership
(U.S. operation of Grant Thornton
International)
Revenue: $635 million (calendar year
04)
No. of Employees: 3,923
No. of Offices: 44

KEY COMPETITORS

Deloitte & Touche
Ernst & Young
KPMG
PricewaterhouseCoopers

EMPLOYMENT CONTACT

Visit the "careers" section of the
firm's web site:
www.grantthornton.com/careers

Visit the Vault Finance Career Channel at **www.vault.com/finance** — with
insider firm profiles, message boards, the Vault Finance Job Board and more.

VAULT CAREER LIBRARY   99

J.H. Cohn LLP

75 Eisenhower Parkway
Roseland, NJ 07068
Phone: (973) 228-3500
Fax: (973) 228-0330
www.jhcohn.com

DEPARTMENTS

Accounting and Auditing
Benefits Consulting
Business Investigation Services
Cost Segregation Studies
Estate Planning
Executive Search
Financing Services
Internal Audit Services
International Business
Management Consulting
Mergers and Acquisitions
Networking and Software Solutions
Special Outsource Services
Tax Services
Wealth Management

THE STATS

CEO: Thomas J. Marino
Employer Type: Private partnership
Revenue: $103.1 million (FYE 1/04)
No. of Employees: 600+
No. of Offices: 9

EMPLOYMENT CONTACT

Cecilia Kash-Valenti
Director of Human Resources – New
Jersey
Phone: (973) 228-3500
E-mail: ckash-valenti@jhcohn.com

Stanley Stempler
Director of Human Resources – New
York
Phone: (212) 297-0400
E-mail: sstempler@jhcohn.com
www.jhcohn.com/careers.cfm

KPMG LLP

345 Park Avenue
New York, NY 10154
Phone: (212) 758-9700
Fax: (202) 758-9819
www.us.kpmg.com

DEPARTMENTS

Assurance
Tax

Visit the Vault Finance Career Channel at **www.vault.com/finance** — with
insider firm profiles, message boards, the Vault Finance Job Board and more.

VAULT CAREER LIBRARY   101

LarsonAllen (Larson, Allen, Weishair & Co., LLP)

220 South Sixth Street
Suite 300
Minneapolis, MN 55402-1436
Phone: (612) 376-4500
Fax: (612) 376-4850
www.larsonallen.com

SERVICES

Assurance
Accounting
Benefit Services
Business Valuation
Executive Search
Industry-specific Consulting
Information Security
Litigation Services
Risk Assurance and Consulting
Tax

THE STATS

CEO: Gordon A. Viere
Employer Type: Private partnership
Revenue: $90.6 million (FYE 10/03)
No. of Employees: 750
No. of Offices: 7

EMPLOYMENT CONTACT

www.larsonallen.com/aboutus/hr_main.asp

McGladrey & Pullen LLP

3600 American Blvd. West
Third Floor
Bloomington, MN 55431-1082
Phone: (952) 835-9930
Fax: (952) 921-7702
www.mcgladrey.com

DEPARTMENTS

Accounting
Audit
Consulting
Human Resources
Information Technology
Insurance
International Tax
Sales and Marketing
Tax
Technical
Telecommunications

THE STATS

Chairman, CEO and Managing Partner:
William D. (Bill) Travis
Employer Type: Private partnership
Revenue: $586.0 million (FYE 4/04)
No. of Offices: 92
No. of Employees: 4,000 +

KEY COMPETITORS

BDO Seidman
Deloitte & Touche
Grant Thornton

EMPLOYMENT CONTACT

Human Resources Department
McGladrey & Pullen
3600 American Blvd. West
Third Floor
Bloomington, MN 55431-1082
Fax: (952) 921-7702

Moss Adams LLP

1001 Fourth Avenue
31st Floor
Seattle, WA 98154-1199
Phone: (206) 223-1820
Fax: (206) 652-2098
www.mossadams.com

DEPARTMENTS

Assurance Services
Consulting Services (Business
Consulting, Claims Resolution,
Information Technology, Litigation
Services, Mergers & Acquisitions,
Personal Wealth Services, Research
Services, Risk Management,
Royalty Compliance, SEC/Corporate
Finance Services, Valuation
Services)
Tax Services

THE STATS

Chairman and CEO: Rick Anderson
Employer Type: Private partnership
Revenue: $181.0 million (FYE 12/03)
No. of Employees: 1,319 (including
183 partners)
No. of Offices: 18

KEY COMPETITORS

BDO Seidman
Deloitte & Touche
Ernst & Young
Grant Thornton
KPMG
McGladrey & Pullen
PricewaterhouseCoopers

EMPLOYMENT CONTACT

Shannon Urion
Senior Recruitment Manager
Phone: (206) 223-1820
E-mail: recruiter@mossadams.com
www.mossadams.com/careers

Parente Randolph LLC

Two Penn Center Plaza
Suite 1800
Philadelphia PA 19102-1725
Phone: (215) 972.0701
Fax: (215) 563.4925
www.parentenet.com

DEPARTMENTS

Assurance Services
Business Reorganization
Corporate Finance
Forensic Accounting & Litigation
    Services
HR Services
Management Consulting
Retirement & Estate Planning
Tax Services
Technology

THE STATS

CEO: Robert Ciaruffoli
Employer Type: Private partnership
Revenue: $44.9 million (FYE 10/02)
No. of Employees: 350+
No. of Offices: 18

EMPLOYMENT CONTACT

www.parentenet.com/careers.htm

Plante & Moran PLLC

27400 Northwestern Highway
Southfield, MI 48034
Phone: (248) 352-2500
Fax: (248) 352-0018
www.plantemoran.com

DEPARTMENTS

Accounting
Consulting
Financial Advisors
International Business
Mergers & Acquisitions
Technology

PricewaterhouseCoopers LLP

300 Madison Avenue
New York, NY 10017
Phone: (646) 471-3000
Fax: (813) 286-6000
www.pwcglobal.com/us

SERVICES

Advisory
Assurance
Tax

THE STATS

Chairman, Senior Partner, U.S.: Dennis
M. Nally
Employer Type: Private partnership
(U.S. arm of PricewaterhouseCoopers)
Revenue (Global): $16.3 billion (FYE
6/04)
No. of Employees: 23,000
No. of Offices: 85

KEY COMPETITORS

Deloitte & Touche
Ernst & Young
KPMG

EMPLOYMENT CONTACT

See www.pwc.com/uscareers

Reznick Group, P.C.

7700 Old Georgetown Road
Suite 400
Bethesda, MD 20814-6224
Phone: (301) 652-9100
Fax: (301) 652-1848
www.reznickgroup.com

SERVICES

Audit and Accounting
Business Valuation and Transaction
   Advisory Services
Cost Segregation
Forensic Accounting and Litigation
   Support Services
Government Services
Internal Audit
Management Advisory Services
Real Estate Transaction Structuring
   and Advisory Services
Sarbanes-Oxley Act Section 404
   Compliance
State and Local Tax
Tax Consulting
Wealth Management

THE STATS

Managing Principal: Kenneth E.
Baggett
Employer Type: Private partnership
Revenue: $90.8 million (FYE 9/04)
No. of Employees: 819
No. of Offices: 5

EMPLOYMENT CONTACT

See the "careers" section of
www.reznickgroup.com

Rothstein, Kass & Co.

85 Livingston Avenue
Roseland, NJ 07068
Phone: (973) 994-6666
Fax: (973) 740-1818
www.rkco.com

DEPARTMENTS

Accounting and Auditing
Coaching and Affiliation
Due Diligence
Litigation Support/Forensic
Accounting
Management Advisory Services
Mergers and Acquisitions
Personal Financial Planning
SEC Services
Tax Planning and Compliance

THE STATS

Managing Principals: Steve Kass &
Howard Altman
Employer Type: Private company
Revenue: $71.7 million (FYE 12/03)
No. of Employees: 460
No. of Offices: 8

EMPLOYMENT CONTACT

New York/New Jersey
Attn: Human Resources- WS
85 Livingston Avenue
Roseland, NJ 07068
Fax: (973) 740-1818
E-mail: hr-east@rkco.com

Beverly Hills/San Francisco/Dallas
Attn: Human Resources-WS
9171 Wilshire Boulevard, Suite 500
Beverly Hills, CA 90210
Fax: (310) 273-6649
E-mail: hr-west@rkco.com

Schenck Business Solutions

200 E. Washington Street
P.O. Box 1739
Appleton, WI   54912-1739
Phone: (920) 731-8111; (800)
236-2246
Fax: (920) 731-8037
www.schencksolutions.com

DEPARTMENTS

Accounting & Auditing
Business Consulting
Estate & Trust Planning
HR Consulting
International Business Solutions
Investment Management
Mergers & Acquisitions
Payroll Services
Retirement Plan Administration
Tax Planning & Compliance
Technology Solutions
Valuations & Litigation

THE STATS

President: William D. Goodman
Employer Type: Private company
Revenue: $52.0 million (FYE 10/03)
No. of Employees: 500+
No. of Offices: 11

EMPLOYMENT CONTACT

www.schencksolutions.com/careers.htm

Virchow, Krause & Company LLP

10 Terrace Court
Madison, WI 53718
Phone: (608) 249-6622
www.virchowkrause.com

SERVICES

Accounting, Assurance & Advisory
Consulting
Employee Benefits
Insurance
International
Investment Management
Litigation & Valuation
Sarbanes-Oxley
Software & Systems
Staffing
Tax
Wealth Management

THE STATS

CEO: Tim Christen
Employer Type: Private partnership
Revenue: $136.3 million (FYE 5/04)
No. of Employees: 850+
No. of Offices: 11

EMPLOYMENT CONTACT

careers.virchowkrause.com

Visit the Vault Finance Career Channel at **www.vault.com/finance** — with
insider firm profiles, message boards, the Vault Finance Job Board and more.

VAULT CAREER LIBRARY   111

Weiser LLP

135 West 50th Street
New York, NY 10020
Phone: (212) 812-7000
Fax: (212) 375-6888
www.weiserllp.com

DEPARTMENTS

Auditing and Accounting
Business Consulting
Business Investigation Services
Corporate Finance
Executive Search
IT Consulting
Insurance
International Services
Investment Advisory Services
Litigation Support
Outsourcing Management
Pension, Benefits and
  Compensation
Personal Financial Planning
Private Client Services
Royalty & Contract Compliance
SEC Services
Tax Planning and Compliance
Trusts and Estate
Turnaround and Bankruptcy

THE STATS

Managing Partner: Andy Cohen
Employer Type: Private partnership
Revenue: $53.0 million (FYE 12/02)
No. of Employees: 350+
No. of Offices: 3

EMPLOYMENT CONTACT

John Porricelli
Director of Human Resources
Weiser LLP
135 West 50th Street
New York, NY 10020
E-mail: jporricelli@weiserllp.com

Wipfli LLP

11 Scott Street
Wausau, WI 54403
Phone: (715) 845-3111
Fax: (715) 842-7272
www.wipfli.com

DEPARTMENTS

Management/Business Consulting
Accounting, Auditing and Tax
Strategic Business Planning
Human Resource Consulting
Business Valuation Services
Family Business Services
Marketing Consulting
Information Technology and
    Business Improvement Services
Information Systems Planning,
    Design and Implementation
Business Process Improvement
Accounting Systems
Implementation and Support
Electronic Commerce and
    Groupware Solutions
Executive Information and Decision
    Support Systems
Financial Planning and Tax Services
Retirement and Estate Planning
Employee Benefit Plan
Administration and Consulting
Personal Financial Planning
Tax Planning and Strategies

THE STATS

Managing Partner: Greg Barber
Employer Type: Private partnership
Revenue: $76.0 million (FYE 5/04)
No. of Employees: 600+
No. of Offices: 18

EMPLOYMENT CONTACT

www.wipfli.com/wipfli/careers

Visit the Vault Finance Career Channel at **www.vault.com/finance** — with
insider firm profiles, message boards, the Vault Finance Job Board and more.

VAULT CAREER LIBRARY   113

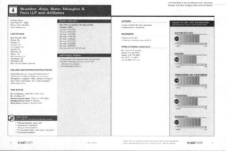

APPENDIX

APPENDIX

Glossary

Accelerated depreciation: Any depreciation method that writes off depreciable costs more quickly than the ordinary straight-line method.

Account payable: A liability that results from a purchase of goods or services on open account.

Accounting: The process of identifying, recording, summarizing and reporting economic information to decision makers.

Accounting controls: The methods and procedures for authorizing transactions, safeguarding assets and ensuring the accuracy of financial controls.

Accounting Principles Board (APB): The predecessor of the Financial Accounting Standards Board (FASB).

Accounting system: A set of records, procedures and equipment that routinely deals with the events affecting the financial performance and position of the entity.

Account receivable: An amount owed to a company by customers as a result of delivering goods or services and extending credit in the ordinary course of business.

Accrual basis: Accounting method that recognizes the impact of transactions on the financial statements in the time periods when revenues and expenses occur.

Accrue: To accumulate a receivable or payable during a given period even though no explicit transaction occurs.

Accumulated depreciation: The cumulative sum of all depreciation recognized since the date of acquisition of the particular assets described.

Administrative controls: All methods and procedures that facilitate management planning and control of operations.

American Institute of Certified Public Accountants (AICPA): The leading organization of the auditors of corporate financial reports.

Allowance for doubtful accounts: A contra asset account that measures the amount of receivables estimated to be uncollected.

Amortization: When referring to long-lived assets, it usually means the allocation of the costs of intangible assets to the periods that benefit from these assets.

Annual report: A combination of financial statements, management discussion and analysis, and graphs and charts that is provided annually to investors.

APB Opinions: A series of 31 opinions of the Accounting Principles Board, many of which are still in effect.

Assets: Economic resources that are expected to benefit future cash inflows or help reduce future cash outflows.

Audit: An examination of transactions and financial statements made in accordance with generally accepted auditing standards.

Audit committee: A committee of the board of directors that oversees the internal accounting controls, financial statements and financial affairs of the corporation.

Auditor: A person that examines the information used by managers to prepare the financial statements and attests to the credibility of those statements.

Auditor's opinion: A report describing the auditor's examination of transactions and financial statements, included with the financial statements in an annual report issued by the corporation.

Bad debt expense: The cost of granting credit that arises from uncollectible accounts.

Balance sheet (statement of financial condition): A financial statement that shows the financial status of a business entity at a particular moment in time.

Balance sheet equation: Assets = Liabilities + Owners' Equity.

Book value (carrying value): The balance of an account shown on the books, net of any contra accounts.

Capital: A term used to identify owners' equities for proprietorships and partnerships.

Capitalization (capital structure): Owners' equity plus long-term debt.

Capitalized: A cost that is added to an asset account, as distinguished from being expensed immediately.

Cash basis: Accounting method that recognizes the impact of transactions on the financial statements only when cash is received or disbursed.

Cash equivalents: Highly liquid short-term investments that can easily be converted to cash.

Cash flows from financing activities: The third major section of the statement of cash flows, describing flows to and from providers of capital.

Cash flows from investing activities: The second major section of the statement of cash flows, describing the purchases and sales of plant, property, equipment and other long-lived assets.

Cash flows from operating activities: The first major section of the statement of cash flows, showing the cash effects of transactions that affect the income statement.

Certified public accountant (CPA): In the United States, a person earns this designation by a combination of education, qualifying experience and the passing of a written examination.

Common stock: Stock representing the class of owners having a "residual" ownership of a corporation.

Conservatism: Selecting accounting methods and treatments that yield lower net income, lower assets, and/or lower stockholders' equity.

Consolidated statements: Combinations of the financial positions and earnings of the parent company with those of various subsidiaries into an overall report as if they were a single entity.

Contingent liability: A potential liability, often off-balance sheet, which depends on the occurrence of a future event arising out of a past transaction.

Contra account: A separate but related account that offsets or is a deduction from a companion account.

Cost of goods available for sale: Sum of beginning inventory and current year purchases.

Cost of goods sold (cost of sales): The original acquisition cost of the inventory that was sold to customers during the reporting period.

Cost recovery: The concept by which some purchases of goods or services are recorded as assets because their costs are expected to be recovered in the form of cash inflows, or reduced cash outflows, in future periods.

Credit: An entry or balance on the right side of an account.

Current assets: Cash plus assets that are expected to be converted to cash, sold or consumed during the next 12 months (or within the normal operating cycle if longer than a year).

Current liabilities: Liabilities that fall due within the coming year (or within the normal operating cycle if longer than a year).

Current ratio (working capital ratio): Current assets divided by current liabilities.

Debit: An entry or balance on the left side of an account.

Debt-to-equity ratio: Total liabilities divided by total shareholders' equity.

Depletion: The process of allocating the cost of natural resources to the periods in which the resources are used.

Visit the Vault Finance Career Channel at **www.vault.com/finance** — with insider firm profiles, message boards, the Vault Finance Job Board and more.

VAULT CAREER LIBRARY   **119**

Depreciable value: The amount of the acquisition cost to be allocated as depreciation over the total useful life of an asset. It is the difference between the total acquisition cost and the predicted residual value.

Depreciation: The allocation of the acquisition cost of long-lived or fixed assets to the expense accounts of particular periods that benefit from the use of the assets.

Dilution: Reduction in stockholders' equity per share or earnings per share that arises from changes among shareholders' proportional interests.

Discontinued operations: The termination of a business segment, the results of which are reported separately, net of tax, in the income statement.

Dividend-payout ratio: Common dividends per share divided by earnings per share.

Dividend-yield ratio: Common dividends per share divided by market price per share.

Double-declining-balance depreciation (DDB): The most popular form of accelerated depreciation, computed by doubling the straight-line rate and multiplying the resulting DDB rate by the beginning book value.

Double-entry system: The method usually followed for recording transactions, whereby at least two accounts are always affected by each transaction.

Earnings per share (EPS): Net income divided by average number of common shares outstanding.

EBIT: Earnings before interest and taxes.

EBITDA: Earnings before interest, taxes, depreciation and amortization.

Expenses: Decreases in owners' equity that arise because goods or services are delivered to customers.

Extraordinary items: Items that are unusual in nature and infrequent in occurrence that are shown separately, net of tax, in the income statement.

Financial accounting: The field of accounting that serves external decision makers, such as stockholders, suppliers, banks and government agencies.

Financial Accounting Standards Board (FASB): A private-sector body that determines generally accepted accounting principles in the United States.

Financing activities: Activities that involve obtaining resources as a borrower or issuer of securities and repaying creditors and owners.

First-in, first-out (FIFO): A method of inventory accounting that assigns the cost of the earliest acquired units to cost of goods sold first.

Fiscal year: The year established for accounting purposes.

General ledger: The collection accounts that accumulates the amounts reported in the major financial statements.

Generally Accepted Accounting Principles (GAAP): A term that applies to the broad concepts or guidelines and detailed practices in accounting, including all the conventions, rules and procedures that make up accepted accounting practice.

Goodwill: The excess of the cost of an acquired company over the sum of the fair market value of its identifiable individual assets less the liabilities.

Gross profit (gross margin): The excess of sales revenue over the cost of the inventory that was sold.

Gross sales: Total sales revenue before deducting sales returns and allowances.

Historical cost: The amount originally paid to acquire an asset.

Income statement (statement of earnings): A report of all revenues and expenses pertaining to a specific time period.

Intangible assets: Rights or economic benefits, such as patents, trademarks, copyrights and goodwill, that are not physical in nature.

Internal control: System of checks and balances that assures that all actions occurring within the company are in accordance with organizational objectives.

Inventory: Goods held by a company for the purpose of sale to customers.

Investing activities: Activities that involve (1) providing and collecting cash as a lender or as an owner of securities and (2) acquiring and disposing of plant, property, equipment and other long-term productive assets.

Journal entry: An analysis of the effects of a transaction on the accounts, usually accompanied by an explanation.

Last-in, first-out (LIFO): An inventory method that assigns most recent costs to cost of goods sold.

Ledger: The records for a group of related accounts kept current in a systematic manner.

Liabilities: Economic obligations of the organization to outsiders or claims against its assets by outsiders.

Long-lived assets: Resources held for an extended time, such as land, buildings, equipment, natural resources and patents.

Long-term liabilities: Obligations that fall due beyond one year from the balance sheet date.

Lower-of-cost-or-market method (LCM): The superimposition of a market-price test on an inventory cost method.

Management accounting: The field of accounting that serves internal decision makers, such as top executives, department heads, administrators and people at other levels of management within an organization.

Management's discussion and analysis (MD&A): A required section of annual reports that concentrates on explaining the major changes in the income statement, liquidity and capital resources.

Matching: The recording of expenses in the same time period as the related revenues that are recognized.

Materiality convention: The concept that a financial statement item is material if its omission or misstatement would tend to mislead the reader of the financial statements.

Net income: The remainder after all expenses have been deducted from revenues.

Net sales: Total sales revenue reduced by sales returns and allowances.

Notes payable: Promissory notes that are evidence of a debt and state the payment terms.

Operating activities: Transactions that affect the income statement.

Operating income: Gross profit less all operating expenses.

Outstanding shares: Shares remaining in the hands of shareholders.

Owners' equity: The residual interest in the organization's assets after deducting liabilities.

Paid-in capital: The total capital investment in a corporation by its owners at the inception of the business and subsequently.

Par value: The nominal dollar amount printed on stock certificates.

Permanent differences: Revenue or expense items that are recognized for tax purposes but not recognized for GAAP, or vice versa.

Pretax income: Income before income taxes.

Price-earnings ratio (P-E): Market price per share of common stock divided by earnings per share of common stock.

Private accountants: Accountants who work for businesses, government agencies and other nonprofit organizations.

Public accountants: Accountants who offer services to the general public on a fee basis including auditing, tax work and management consulting.

Recognition: A test for determining whether revenues should be recorded in the financial statement of a given period. To be recognized, revenues must be earned and realized.

Reserve: Has one of three meanings: (1) a restriction of dividend-declaring power as denoted by a specific subdivision of retained income, (2) an offset to an asset, or (3) an estimate of a definite liability of indefinite or uncertain amount.

Residual value (terminal value, salvage value): The amount received from disposal of a long-lived asset at the end of its useful life.

Retained income (retained earnings): Additional owners' equity generated by income.

Revenues (sales): Increases in owners' equity arising from increases in assets received in exchange for the delivery of goods or services to customers.

Special items: Expenses that are large enough and unusual enough to warrant separate disclosure.

Statement of cash flows: A statement that reports the cash receipts and cash payments of an entity during a particular period.

Stockholders' equity (shareholders' equity): Owners' equity of a corporation. The excess of assets over liabilities.

Straight-line depreciation: A method that spreads the depreciable value evenly over the useful life of an asset.

T-account: Simplified version of ledger accounts.

Tangible assets (fixed assets): Physical items that can be seen and touched.

Timing differences (temporary differences): Differences between net income and taxable income that arise because some revenue and expense items are recognized at different times for tax purposes than for reporting purposes.

Treasury stock: A corporation's issued stock that has subsequently been repurchased by the company and not retired.

Trial balance: A list of all accounts in the general ledger with their balances.

Uncollectible accounts (bad debts): Receivables determined to be uncollectible because debtors are unable or unwilling to pay their debts.

Unearned revenue (deferred revenue): Revenue received and recorded before it is earned.

Useful life: The time period over which an asset is depreciated.

Working capital: The excess of current assets over current liabilities.

Write-down: A reduction in the assumed cost of an item in response to a decline in value.

V/\ULT CAREER LIBRARY

About the Authors

Jason Alba: Jason is an MBA graduate from the University of Michigan Business School, where he had concentrations in economics and corporate strategy. He earned a BS in Accounting from New York University's Stern School of Business. Prior to attending Michigan, Jason worked in tax accounting for PricewaterhouseCoopers and Viacom. He also worked in the financial reporting group at J.P. Morgan.

Manisha Bathija: Manisha is a recent MBA graduate from the University of Michigan Business School, where she focused on finance. She also has a BA in Chemistry and a BS in Accounting from Virginia Polytechnic Institute & State University. Prior to attending Michigan, Manisha worked as an auditor in the Vienna, Virginia office of Arthur Andersen LLP.

Matthew Thorton: Matt is a Senior Editor at Vault. He graduated from Harvard with a BA in English. Previously, he was an editor at Random House.

Competition on the Street – and beyond – is heating up. With the finance job market tightening, you need to be your best.

We know the finance industry. And we've got experts that know the finance environment standing by to review your resume and give you the boost you need to snare the financial position you deserve.

Finance Resume Writing and Resume Reviews

- Have your resume reviewed by a practicing finance professional.

- For resume writing, start with an e-mailed history and 1- to 2-hour phone discussion. Our experts will write a first draft, and deliver a final draft after feedback and discussion.

- For resume reviews, get an in-depth, detailed critique and rewrite within TWO BUSINESS DAYS.

Finance Career Coaching

Have a pressing finance career situation you need Vault's expert advice with? We've got experts who can help.

- Trying to get into investment banking from business school or other careers?
- Switching from one finance sector to another – for example, from commercial banking to investment banking?
- Trying to figure out the cultural fit of the finance firm you should work for?

"Thank you, thank you, thank you! I would have never come up with these changes on my own!"

– W.B., Associate, Investment Banking, NY

"Having an experienced pair of eyes looking at the resume made more of a difference than I thought."

– R.T., Managing Director, SF

"I found the coaching so helpful I made three appointments!"

– S.B., Financial Planner, NY

For more information go to www.vault.com/finance

VAULT
> the most trusted name in career information™

Decrease your T/NJ Ratio
(Time to New Job)

Use the Internet's most targeted job search tools for finance professionals.

Vault Finance Job Board

The most comprehensive and convenient job board for finance professionals. Target your search by area of finance, function, and experience level, and find the job openings that you want. No surfing required.

VaultMatch Resume Database

Vault takes match-making to the next level: post your resume and customize your search by area of finance, experience and more. We'll match job listings with your interests and criteria and e-mail them directly to your inbox.